The Eyes Are Sunlight

The Eyes Are Sunlight is one woman's moving story of her personal journey through grief—a true story of coping and finally growing, after the death of her husband from cancer.

It is a story of living through grief and learning to understand and accept its grace—of looking back and recognizing the presence of God in the worst of times.

The book contains superb insights into the human emotions and feelings which precede and accompany grief. One or the other of those insights is bound to hit home—to touch a personal nerve of experience. The author's reflections are often illustrated by examples and words all too familiar.

The Eyes Are Sunlight is a true love story, a powerful testimony of faith, lovingly written and deeply moving.

Shirley Cecilia Koers is a native of India who currently makes her home in Perth, Australia. She is a retired school teacher.

D0725878

Eyes I dare not meet in dreams
In death's dream kingdom
These do not appear:
There, the eyes are
Sunlight on a broken column

T. S. Eliot—*The Hollow Men*

THE EYES ARE SUNLIGHT

THE EYES ARE SUNLIGHT

A Journey Through Grief

BY SHIRLEY KOERS

Phoenix Press

WALKER AND COMPANY
New York

Large Print Edition by arrangement with Ave Maria Press

Permissions and credits:

Excerpt from "The Hollow Men" by T.S. Eliot, from
Collected Poems 1909–1962, reprinted by permission of
Harcourt, Brace, Jovanovich, Inc., New York (1963), and
Faber and Faber, Ltd., London.

Excerpts from *The Prophet*, by Kahlil Gibran, reprinted by
permission of Alfred A. Knopf. Inc. Copyright 1923 by Kahlil
Gibran and renewed 1951 by Administrators C.T.A. of Kahlil
Gibran Estate and Mary G. Gibran.

Library of Congress Cataloging-in-Publication Data

Koers, Shirley.
  The eyes are sunlight.

  Originally published: Notre Dame, IN:
Ave Maria Press, c1986.
  1. Bereavement—Religious aspects—Christianity.
2. Koers, Jack. 3. Koers, Shirley. I. Title.
[BV4908.K57 1987]   248.8'6   86-30667
ISBN 0-8027-2586-4

Printed in the United States of America

First Large Print Edition, 1987
Walker and Company
720 Fifth Avenue
New York, New York 10019

Contents

My Thanks

To:
Father Michael G. O'Hagan, priest of the Society of Mary, who is permitted to forget the events described here but whose part in them will never be forgotten;
Kath Clark, who pressed me to write in the first place and so set the seal on the requests that came from friends overseas and on my own conviction that I had to do it;
Gay Dingle, who contributed some very poignant recollections of Jack and through whom he and I met;
Warren Clode, who read the initial 60 pages of the first draft of my manuscript and gave me the wonderful idea that in a Rembrandt etching the whole is more than the sum of its parts;
Anne Symons, for introducing me to the works of the Lebanese poet Kahlil Gibran.
Also, those who helped this book to grow

by their sensitive reading of the various drafts; and those unnamed others who, as part of me, are an implicit part of it. They will never know how often a chance word of theirs became for me a channel of light and understanding, and how much this book owes to the beauty and meaning they brought to my life. I thank, bless and love them.

To
Jacobus
(Rest in Peace)
through whom I learned
the meaning
of love

Foreword

DURING my first year away from India in my new country, Australia (1970), I met a publisher from Melbourne who was looking for writers. "All we want is a very human story," he told me.

I had always believed I would write a book one day, and there was plenty to write about. There were the experiential years working with Mother Teresa in Calcutta and the unforgettable teaching years in the magnificent Darjeeling-Himalaya region of north Bengal on the threshold of tiger, leopard and elephant country.

But the "embrace of life and death," to quote from a letter, had not yet been given. The story was still unborn.

That story began when a powerful experience in my life entered my psyche, an event after which nothing could ever be as it had been before. The compulsion to write about it left me without peace and I made a labored, abortive start. Chronology totally escaped me and somehow narrative failed. Only when I hit upon the prose-poem presentation was I able to write at all. Fortunately I did not know how difficult the task was going to be or I might never have begun.

As I tried to share this experience on paper, off and on five years ago, I knew only that love is bound up with pain and that nothing I had ever lived through could equal it for punishment. Now I have slowly discovered that love heals. It puts you together again and makes you shining and new. It is a kind of redemption. You are now paid for by your own tears and you belong not to yourself but wholly to your love.

And so this book became immeasurably more than a journey through grief, and so much bigger than just Jack and me. Faith is its real theme. Even if in this state of ambiguity you don't understand the meaning and miracle in the mystery, it is there. You are part of the whole, and though its full unbearable beauty is still hidden from your eyes, what you have glimpsed from the depths is enough—

more than enough—to win your total trust.

I am no potential artist like Jack, but at least I know an artist must paint what *he* sees. So too someone who attempts to write must put aside the anticipated reactions of known and unknown people and write with sincerity according to what *she* wants to say. I must give you ourselves as we are, or not at all. I must present our experience as it happened, or it is not worth sharing.

In the last six years I have become more and more aware of the spiritual needs around me—the life-hunger, the searching, the delight in sharing at a deep level. There is no doubt what people really want in their secret selves. They are sick of what is hollow, false and sterile. That is why I have written with and from my heart, boldly, not for a market, or for my friends. I have written the way I have because for me there was no other way I could have written.

The events containing this inward journey took place during the ten years I lived in New Zealand, and it was there I wrote the book. They became the most growing years of my life and I will never be able to think of New Zealand without a feeling of unshed tears for the friends and country I have left behind—the country that gave me Jack. I have learned more about love from death than from "the myriad forms of life those stars unroll." When the negative elements have been purified, love burns like a refining flame. The tears of remorse for failures in love can be lifelong, however, like Peter's—or Judas's.

This book is not offered as any kind of guidebook for the bereaved. It is simply my own response to the challenge of personal grief. While every death is unique in the way it is experienced, what I have written about, believing it was meant to be shared, is the uniqueness of my experience *to me*.

Of all the secrets of the fourth dimension (time) death is the most transforming in its power to strengthen and purify because of all the love unleashed by all the pain. If you can get past the crushing and bruising you will find your heart opening wide, setting you free from the fear of death because you have looked into the eyes of Life, that shining inner reality of love laid bare by the healing pain. For me this is a vastness, a propulsion of being toward a goal, a stepping out on to a narrow ledge at the top of a deep chasm, a longing, an unshakable faith that in the end the victory belongs to love, not death.

This is the experience I would like to share with you, if I can. This book is not a sad one though it contains a lot of heartbreak. It is lovingly written but is free from sentimentality. And it is not a biography of Jack. After all, I was married to him for only two and a half years. Jack wanted me to write a book, just as I wanted him to paint pictures; but having no idea he could be special enough to be the subject he would have said in mock disdain: "Oh ... come on, darling!"

Yet his eyes would have twinkled.

Shirley C. Koers
Perth, Australia

Part One

Jack ... The Happening

For what is it to die but to stand naked in the wind and to melt into the sun?

And what is it to cease breathing but to free the breath from its restless tides, that it may rise and expand and seek God unencumbered?

Only when you drink from the river of silence shall you indeed sing.

And when you have reached the mountain top, then shall you begin to climb.

And when the earth shall claim your limbs, then shall you truly dance.

Kahlil Gibran—*The Prophet*

1

Signed Jack and Shirley

HAPPY ARE THEY WHO ARE CALLED TO THE LORD'S SUPPER.

THESE are the words I have put on Jack's headstone.

The time of his dying was the time of a spiritual dinner party, a sacrificial banquet, a love-feast, an agape. He received the Lord's body and blood for the first time—and it was the last time too, in spite of all my hopes.

We are dressing to go to the evening Mass being celebrated at our special request for Jack's first holy communion. Jack looks so beautiful, as if he were

King Solomon wearing the diadem with which his mother crowned him on his wedding day, on the day of his heart's joy. He is wearing the suit we bought in London last year, a rich olive green-brown (was ever a garment so little yet so fully worn?). As always I have brushed his shoulders, arranged his tie (the wedding one), and kissed him approvingly. He has about him the impenetrable stillness and silence of another world. His cheeks are glowing, his eyes steady.

Your eyes are the color of the sea, I once said to him, looking from their blue-green sparkle to the South Pacific ahead of us. He was at once overcome with boyish bashfulness and we had to deflect the conversation to less emotional issues.

Do you remember, my darling?

Now I am afraid to look into his eyes, yet I do. They are vibrant and intelligent still, they know me, they smile, they speak love, they are brighter than a new dawn breaking. Be prepared for personality change, the hospital has warned me. You never know with a brain tumor. . . .

But there is no sign of tumor, nothing more sinister than a weakened grip and a mouth drooping at one corner. His personality, if anything, is at its sweetest. He is altogether lovable. And he can still move freely and easily with the help of drugs (we are spared the paralysis till just before the end). Yet the tumor is so big they cannot treat it, they tell me. Man has travelled in outer space and been covered with moondust, and this sinuous core of pulsing death defies and defeats all our sciences!

He has lost part of a lung already in the struggle to save his life, but now they have admitted their helplessness in the face of probable liver damage and malignancy even in his bones.

Dear God, he looks too well and beautiful to die.

This is Jack's day, a "day that the Lord has made," as we are singing now. We will "rejoice and be glad in it" the way we did 30 months ago when the college girls sang it at our wedding and their happy guitars and voices gladdened our lifelong vows.

The stars fall away behind us like

showers of fireflies as our cradle planet journeys in silence and endlessness carrying Jack through umbilical time past uncounted, unknowing worlds to a new home and all the lost beauties of the world and all the vanished species. For with you, Lord, is the fountain of life.

There is great pain between us, the ageless pain of death and life contending over love, over separation, over loss, over Nature's inexorable law. This time round it is our turn.

The camera—load the camera. Take a photograph, my mind urges. *No*, my heart responds. Nothing can contain this moment, this supreme moment, it is created for remembering.

The college library is crowded with people from the parish and nearly all our friends. Here love is the bond, and differing creeds and philosophies go into the melting pot as we unite in this heart-warming celebration for Jack. But the real celebration is less than 48 hours away and this is only the prelude. Thank you for coming, I am so grateful to see you.

Our voices are gently crooning:

We are gathering together unto him
We are gathering together unto him
Unto him shall the gathering of the
    people be
We are gathering together unto him.

Jack and I are seated in special arm-chairs directly in front of the altar table. He, serene and controlled as always, I, taut with anguish and expectation, my throat constricted and burning—surely that's the taste of blood? For eight months we have fought for his life on the battleground of his body—no, we are not defeated. It is a new phase of victory. I have now come with unshakable confidence to the Lord of our living and our dying, and this gives meaning to every word we are singing to the loving being whom Jesus called Abba.

Gracious Father, gracious Father
We're so glad to be your children
Gracious Father
And we lift our hearts before you
As a token of our love
Gracious Father, gracious Father

Shirley . . . (our parish priest is asking in words I do not remember if I would accept the Lord's will, whatever the outcome, before I prayed for Jack's healing)?

Yes, I answer.

Yes, but only with my lips. In my heart is the reservation that it is unthinkable he would refuse me. (Hadn't I come back from our final hospital journey refusing to accept death—believing I would wrest that miracle from God?) If faith is the condition for miracles then this one must be mine by right—or are his miracles only for others and not for us? Not for me?

He who drew bottomless complexity out of the formless void, who makes the stars career from zone to zone of the limitless heavens like the most capricious of trapeze artists, who knows each bud of spring, each bird by the thousand names in a thousand languages—he can make Jack whole with the wholeness of original homo sapiens who lifted his eyes to the heavens and knew the ONE WHO IS. There is no difference in the Lord's sight between one day and a thousand years. With *this* confidence I approach him, built on Jesus' own promise to do whatever we ask for in his name so that the Father's glory would be shown through the Son.

On the altar, burning brightly, is Jack's candle, lighted by me. The wooden candlestick that snugly holds it is the work of his own hands, turned on his brother Bas' lathe in Holland, too perfect a piece of work to look like what it is: his first bit of turning. Indeed his only one. Who would have thought that seemingly chance attempt would have so much significance? Unspoken, unwritten messages everywhere. . . .

Elizabeth Barrett Browning said it best (or was it Robert?):

Earth's crammed with heaven,
And every common bush afire with
    God;
And only he who sees takes off his
    shoes.
The rest sit round it
And pluck blackberries.

To look at it you'd think it would

burn on forever, and so it will, neither sea nor sky ever able to extinguish it. But Jack's life is ebbing to a close.

―――――――――

The ritual sacrifice begins: first the sorry part. Have mercy. Have mercy. Darling, I have warned Jack earlier, I am going to make a public act of reconciliation, so don't be sad or alarmed. I take his hand and I now say to the Lord and to all his people:

O loving Father, have mercy on all the angry words I have unthinkingly said to Jack. You know I didn't mean them, he knows I didn't mean them, and I know I didn't mean them, but I said them, Lord. You have forgiven me, I know. Please help me to forgive myself. Lord have mercy.

On my left is Jack's stepdaughter Raewyn, crying throughout, and on Jack's right are his younger brother Hans and his eldest sister Maartje who have travelled to be with us. The assembly is now singing to the Holy Spirit calling down his peace.

> Sweep over my soul, sweep over
>   my soul
> Sweet Spirit sweep over my soul
> My rest is complete as I sit at his
>   feet
> Sweet Spirit sweep over my soul

Before we move deeper into the sacrifice there is a time for asking and for saying thank you. The heart is big with gratitude, the broken mind is lifted up. The miracle of being, of having loved, of knowing that inside life's darkest enigmas meaning is preciously locked away for future unfolding—these are gifts that gleam like tiny mirrors by the million in the "awesome wonder" of the worlds his "hands have made."

How fast the minutes go while the years hardly move, somewhat like the near and distant views from the window of a train. My mind goes back to another scene, to only yesterday, and to another altar, in a church, before which Jack and I stood exchanging rings.... Thank you. Thank you.

9

We are coming to the big moment. Holy Holy. Holy Holy.... This is my body which will be given up for you.... This is the cup of my blood....

He is Lord. He is Lord.
He is risen from the dead and he
    is Lord.
Every knee shall bow, every tongue
    confess
That Jesus Christ is Lord.

Lord, let my Jack *live*. You can take away all the sickness destroying his body ... you can make him completely better, as if he had never been ill. If the doctors could have helped him any more I would have gone to them, but your power to theirs is like the teeming galaxies to a grain of sand.

The cancer is virulent and vicious. Eight months ago our world was frozen by shock when the shadow on his right lung was given a dreaded name. We had only just moved into "our" house, just spent six frantically busy weeks redecorating and settling in, so happy the search was over at last—we thought it would be our home. But no, on this earth we have no lasting home to settle in, owning ourselves no better than strangers and exiles. He has had cancer cells in his blood at least 10 to 15 years, the radiotherapist informed me. It takes that long to build a half-inch tumor.

Oh thank you for telling me this—you don't know what it means to me. All this time I have been thinking it is all my fault. Memories of my touchiness besiege and stone me, incidents so normal in the light of day but so magnified in grief; they have all coalesced into cruelty, inhumanity and aggression till *I killed him* burns into my mind like a litany of fire.

His medical report may say smoking has brought him to this (40 to 60 cigarettes a day during a past tragic period of his life), but I think I know better. To some extent it is smoking, and I think it is also his painting trade and we are reaping withered fruits already sown, but most of all I think it is me. For 10 to 15 years it wasn't activated until I came along and ripened the dormant seeds of decay.

The radiotherapist listens to this self-accusation like the most benign of father confessors, compassion flowing out of him. He has seen it all before ... the overwhelming, crushing guilt of loved ones punishing themselves in the intensity of their misery, their pain and self-blame inseparable from their love. If you persist in thinking this, he warns, you will make yourself very very ill. If family tensions were the cause of cancer, then everyone would have it. This is an organic cancer, not a psychosomatic one.

But the devastation is too deep for present alleviation and there is no comfort for me, my mind full of pointing fingers—cranks who persist in labeling cancer "psychosomatic," unaware that cancer-causing agents in all the world's industrial chemicals have made it the largest killer after heart disease. The grief-impaled mind casts desperately and often irrationally around for some rational explanation of the enormity of total physical destruction—vitality gone, talents gone, charm, quirks, u-nique matching of body and mind, all gone, blotted out past hope of recall as if they had never been.

Lord, am *I* the cause of this—*so unteachable* that you couldn't have found another way? I didn't appreciate him enough, that's why you are taking him from me. All this suffering is because of my selfishness.

The worst was that we didn't know about the tumor. I took him to the doctor when the vomiting and headaches began but we didn't know about the tumor till a month later when the visiting cancer specialist prescribed a brain-scan, in case a "seedling from Jack's lung" had gone up to his brain, he said (in the tone of "nice day, isn't it"). I remember laughing (in mirthless terror) to reassure Jack: The specialist must be crazy, darling.

O Lord, please hear my prayer. Hear my prayer. What more can I have done that I have not done? I thought we had eaten all the right things, wholesome food, a balanced diet. Is it a theme for glory to cut down the abstemious and allow the wayward to thrive?

I thought he was getting better and

I treated him accordingly, without too much fuss and with too little sensitivity. But he was getting worse. Perhaps everyone else realized it except me.... Can I blame the doctors for not telling me, or was it my own crass stupidity? I will say their silence made a lifeline out of a shred of hope in my mind and I even believed the chest specialist who said at the beginning: We give him another 20 years at least. I am now a statistic of the blatantly sanguine who "fall for the myth of survival" and pigheadedly believe that miracles cure cancer. (*I know they do.*)

He is better prepared for the inevitable than I am because there was no chink at all in my massive fortress of denial. I have been treating him like a well man because I believed he would get well—but he was *dying*. How can I live with this?

When it was too late—that is, from my point of view—they told me what they must have known all along: lung cancer patients "go very fast because the secondary is usually brain tumor." Jack was doomed because we didn't catch the primary in time. He didn't believe in checkups or anything like that, so while we were holidaying in Europe the year before, his lung was already being slowly strangled—and there was not even one little cough to warn us.

At the time of the chest operation the full reality and all the possibilities were spared me so in the short term we hoped, and that was a good thing after all. They were in effect telling me the perfect way: gradually, gently and kindly . . . but who can spare me suffering now in the long term when Jack is gone and I am alone with my thoughts?

Then we found out about the tumor less than three weeks before his death and I knew for me it was too late. Could anyone give me back the opportunities for anything I might have left ungiven and undone because I didn't know? Mercifully, a few months before he went, some good angel prompted the words to be spoken: I need you, darling—I can't live without you— please don't leave me. But on the whole I behaved as if every day were every-day, when I could have been making

15

a lit-up one for eternal remembering.

Now we are finished with all these doctors. They are very kind and capable, but they are not God. Jack has chosen to come home to die. Perhaps I should have brought him home earlier— O God, why didn't I? He would have been spared all those hundreds of X-rays, all that cobalt, and that lung operation with his lung not drying out so that the drainage tubes were hideously inserted six times over. Even now the memory of that martyrdom makes me cringe.

In those last months Jack was suffering all the time—I mean, before the painkillers were prescribed. His head was thumping, he said. Thumping. *And I didn't know*. I knew about the headaches but I didn't know about the tumor—the awful, unmentionable, too real fact. How can I live with this, God? Can't you just let it be a test of faith, a "trial by ordeal"?

Grief is like an iceberg only hinting the tip of one's sorrow, shutting out the melting oceans, hoarding the load, the mountain-weight load, of hidden,

16

inexpressible, forever-petrified tears. If such tears are drilled, tears that can't now be cried, will they ever be stopped again once they are found?

Whatever you ask ... Jesus had said. Ah ... there are strings attached to the promise, golden strings, offering you more than you wanted or bargained for. You think you have asked properly, with faith, humility and resignation, but you secretly tried to pressure God without letting him decide. He may choose to heal in life, or he may choose to heal in death, but he does heal. It isn't your faith that has staggered or failed. On the contrary. Inexplicably it has been greatly strengthened. Who is to say whether the impact of Jack's death and your whole-hearted response to it have not been a more shining witness to faith than an outright cure would have been?

You know in your heart your request has paid God a compliment, glorified him as we say. It has given him the chance of giving you the spirit of your asking, the pearl, not the encasing, the future good, the real blessing. Somehow you are not hurt by the apparent refusal

17

because of the brilliance of the "light denied." Somehow you know the miracle has mysteriously been granted. Within 24 hours your prayers are now taking a different turn, eagerly awaiting the arrival of merciful death even though you had the faith that could move a mountain—let alone a tumor—and he had the power to give you either an instantaneous cure or a gradual arrest. Perhaps I am still experiencing the effect of that day's shared supplication and togetherness. I did, after all, make a day for eternal remembering.

Jack is far away. His heart is not with us any more and no prayer of ours will hold him back. For me there is the aching regret of his newly completed art studio, a dream child dying immediately after birth, which he will never use. But what is it compared to the gallery of the planets whirling like ballerinas and the Lord of all worlds loving him into a masterpiece?

Earthly existence has climaxed its gifts to him by the greatest gift of all, the pearl beyond all price. Spiritual faith in a spiritual kingdom. He can now only go forward with gratitude and hope along the way that all humanity must go, ready or unready. Death is the last evil we must face, not one of us exempted, in the ceaseless lifelong procession of labors, hardships, hurts, disappointments, frustrations, that are the foundation of our inner mansion. Once death itself has been endured there is only life.

Do you believe in the resurrection of the body and life everlasting? Yes—Yes. Jack answered with crisp decisiveness all the questions on faith put to him exactly a week earlier when, at his own request, our priest came to the house to receive him into the church. How do you feel, Jack? Father asked gently. I am in peace, Jack answered. We both sat and wept silently at the greatness of the mystery. The peace that may elude geniuses and millionaires has been given to Jack, pressed down, shaken together, running over, from the uncreated within him whose light now shines away all darkness. God's peace.

Now we are singing:

I am the Bread of Life

He who comes to me shall not
    hunger
He who believes in me shall not
    thirst
No one can come to me, unless
    the Father draws him
And I will raise him up
And I will raise him up
And I will raise him up on the last
    day.

So moving are the words of this sacred song that each time I sing it I am broken afresh, broken by love, by gratitude; broken by the goodness that found a way to answer my prayer beyond my hopes, and gave me more to hold of Jack than anything that has been taken away.

Our celebrant is speaking again. He is telling our friends how much he regrets not being able to give holy communion to those who are not of our faith. I feel my sister-in-law Maartje's longing and I am filled with the pain of our separation.

Jack stands to receive the body and the blood. I receive after him. Behold my

agony. May this chalice pass from me.
But not my will but thine be done.
In silent prayer and faith

We see the Lord, we see the Lord
And he is high and lifted up
And his train fills the temple
He is high and lifted up
And his train fills the temple
The angels cry Holy
The angels cry Holy
The angles cry Holy is the Lord.

Jack has eaten your body and drunk your blood. He has publicly proclaimed his faith in your Eucharist, Lord Jesus. May he live forever, according to your promise. May he rest in peace.

The Mass is over. Jack stays in his place and friends gather round to congratulate him. They know they will not see him again. He and his friends, Norman and Jim, grasp one another's hands. Gay, Norman's wife, said she held back because she felt that that moment belonged to them. To see men weep is hard, for they could not and did not know how to say goodbye. The words are hers.

21

I go round the entire assembly and embrace each person there. Our solicitor's wife tells me how moved she is and her eyes are brimming.

The next day I write a letter to our priest telling him we love him. Then I give it to Jack to sign first. The left half of his brain is not affected so his right hand writes *Jack* firmly. Then beside it I write *Shirley*.

With exquisite sensitivity Father preserved this note and returned it to me before he left four months later to take up his new appointment. All my un-uttered heartbreak is contained in this one priceless autograph.

2

A Time to Die

Your pain is the breaking of the shell
that encloses your understanding.
Even as the stone of the fruit must
    break,
that its heart may stand in the sun,
so must you know pain.
              Kahlil Gibran—*The Prophet*

IF in the scheme of unimagined
possibilities I were to live to
celebrate my centenary, or go on a
voyage to another planet, or witness
some undreamt-of scientific marvel, the
memory I would wish to hold sacred in
every detail would still be that of Jack's
last two days on earth and my own

inadequate, unworthy part in them. When I touch this memory I touch the Infinite, I touch the Mysterious, I touch all being and all loving.

If by picking up a stone in my garden I am physically in touch with every other stone it has touched or will touch until I have touched even the top of the highest mountain and the bottom of the deepest ocean, then with this memory of mine there is nothing that I cannot touch of earth and of heaven because it belongs to both.

Out of the mass and detail of perfectly ordinary actions that became the framework for this memory came something much greater: profound meaning and immense beauty. A creation.

What happened left me with a sense of wonder and awe, a sense of the rightness of the way things had happened and of the perfection of the timing, so that I knew we were not alone, we were tenderly and firmly held, and we were greatly loved.

I will not be the first or the last to hold a dying person in my arms and to see with my own eyes the actual moment of transition. Or to distill with love and gratitude those last days before that beloved presence was removed from its earthly dimension. Countless people know in their heart the gift they have received and their thank you is heard even if it is not spoken.

This book is discouragingly hard to write . . . sometimes I think too hard. I want it to be like a Rembrandt drawing, a heavy stroke here, a delicate line there, the undrawn image in full bloom in the bud. Or like a poem, the fullness and meaning in the reader's own mind making reflections in a lotus pool—too still for peace, too deep for hurt.

This is a spring morning and no other will ever be like it again. Our breakfast table faces east and the sun is climbing the heights. The country-side is so alive that even a fence-post could dance. Yet there is no resentment in me that I should be celebrating death through whose portals Jack will vanish forever. Relinquishment for him has now been accomplished, and there comes a time when the burden of the body needs to be laid down—the stuggle is over.

We are only *here* to go *there*, a smiling visiting stranger told us matter-of-factly in Palmerston North Hospital nearly two weeks ago when we had just learned that beyond question time was finally running out. Mr. Koers, we can give you further treatment if you wish, but it is very drastic and it won't give you more than another two months ....

Thank God Jack chose to come home. Funny, you'd think that life was almost normal.

Let us enjoy the sun, my darling. When it shines for us again I will be with you in the City of Light and the old will be forgotten in the heady wine of the new with all its never-imagined dimensions of living and loving. Tomorrow you will have slipped away, out of reach of all my cherishing as gently as a raindrop into thirsty sand.

Receive this drop of suffering from the ocean of the world's tears. It is my mite, being everything I have.

Everything has *changed* for us—

realization too stark and subtle to convey except in surface words about surface things. Unfinished work must stay unfinished, empty canvases will never be filled, clothes near-new will be worn by others, the garden (irony of ironies) will be my domain; the feeling of "for the last time" pervades everything.

But how do you learn or unlearn in a few hours what you have not learned or have learned in a whole lifetime? How do you carry away a smile to keep it for eternity? Or continue to warm your heart by the light so soon to be extinguished in the eyes that will look at you forever?

All life's familiar things milling around like specks caught in a sunset ray now show up for the fragile things they are, their appeal lost in the night flares of Gethsemane. Familiar things are a wonderful opiate, however, and it is only the unfamiliar that has significance. Before the end of the day this will be one more gift-wrapped meaning growing in my laden arms. But now we admire the manuka tree on our front lawn dropping its pink petals while the bees court it deliriously.

Praise the Lord, Jack says spontaneously. I look at him and repeat his words and I remember ... our five weeks in the capital for surgery where he learned to say and mean it for the first time.

I mean it but find it difficult to say. For all the power in them, words sound so artificial when I use them. Their hidden meanings are too profound for all my tears to wash to brilliance. Elusive like the moth that dematerializes in mid-dance before my very eyes—how often they have been my downfall through impulsiveness or ambiguity or overheatedness.

To die is to be divested of the need for and tyranny of W-O-R-D-S.

Tomorrow has come today but still not made sense of yesterday ... too big to understand until redemption gives me back each broken piece to make a whole, or the next lightning strikes again. Meanwhile we walk slowly together toward the distant sunrise no night, however dark, can hide.

Jack shaves as usual, putters as usual, his merciful four-hourly betamethasone (for which my alarm is constantly set) coordinating his movements and keeping him comfortable. At some stage I bring him a refreshing drink of pure grapefruit juice from our tree, and later a drink of foaming carrot, celery and spinach from the juice extractor.

His pleasure is written all over his face—he's purring, I tease him again as I often teased him in the days when our love was without a care. *Listen* to it! he retorts as usual with good-natured scorn.

Gone are the days of furious bids for independence: Stop treating me like a child! Now he accepts that I can't help mothering him and he is reconciled to being Shirley's baby. (In fact he quite shamelessly adores being spoiled and fussed over.)

Presently I settle him in a deck chair on the front terrace and hand him the transistor radio I bought him in Australia. He toys with it to show his appreciation but I know it holds no interest for him. The things of earth belong to the thoughts of earth and once these thoughts have changed direction, the things of earth are left behind.

While he is sitting there the strangest thing happens . . . suddenly we have the most unusual and unexpected of visitors. A pair of wild ducks wander onto our lawn. Darling, look, they have come to see you. Never before or since have I been honored with such entrancing company, such exuberant aloofness, such friendly distance and disdain!

It is not a casual visit made in passing. They spend all day with us by obvious choice, sitting lovingly under the manuka tree they have singled out, close together, in full view of us, graciously accepting but not needing the bread I crumble and offer them. I have heard of angels in disguise, and these free lovely creatures give my spirits a marvelous lift and leave me wondering again about the spiritual in the material. . . .

Now Jack is puttering again around the house and garden, and this time he disappears for a while into his studio-den. I do not follow him. In the days to come I will read the message, warm as the glow of a candle, heartwrenching as a surgeon's knife, set up in this most special place.

In the evening he goes into the shower calling: Darling, give me a nice towel! I remove the boring ordinary ones and bring out the nicest special ones with all his favorite autumn tones. Does he know he is performing this ritual ablution for the last time?

There was another time, unforgettable because so tender, when he sat in the bath after the cobalt with a little-boy look on his face and I carefully sponged him to avoid burning the treated area. Now when he comes out scrubbed and shining I can't resist the temptation to give him the hero treatment.

Maartje, have you seen Jack's wound? Come over here. Jack acts very coy, pulling his vest up shyly, but he is secretly proud of his huge crescent scar—and well he might be for the courage it took to acquire it. We count the marks of the drainage tubes: *eight* with the original two.

But in the months to come I will be very proud of Jack, very proud that he is so completely himself to the last day even to shaving and showering without help. The wit still bubbles out of him

31

though we can no longer enjoy his final little jokes. Indeed, they almost make me angry because it is so heartrendingly bizarre trying to laugh when humor itself is grief-stricken and laughter has been silenced by tears.

But he will die as he has lived, sunnily, and for that I thank God. he was granted an intelligent death and friends will say to me later: Shirley, you have had your miracle. I know. I know.

When it is getting dark I pull down the blinds, an action I enjoy as the much as letting in the new day early in the morning. Then I turn on the lights, subdued and intimate, and we are surrounded by peace even though there is no joy. Our greatest strength, strangely, is the pain we each suffer on account of the other which forces us to behave as ordinarily as possible so that in spite of ourselves we are as we have always been.

Maartje decided to stay on after last night's service and her presence is very comforting to both of us. She is now in her room and Jack and I are alone for a few minutes before tea. He is sitting in his La-Z-Boy rocker as he has always sat, only this time there is a difference: he will never sit in it again. Then his eyes catch mine as I come into the dining room on my way to the table . . .

You will marry again of course, he says to me very casually, sharing the thought that is lying on his heart. Just as casually I answer: I doubt it, my darling. He seems satisfied. There are no kisses or embraces or tears. I don't know it yet, but these are his last words to me.

Oh my darling, why do I treat you like a stranger? If only I had come to you . . . sat down by you . . . taken your hand. At night when you are alone in the aloneness of sleep I touch your head and cry to the night into which you are going, but face to face I can only look past you as if I did not know or care. Already we are separated by countless timeless eternal years.

Soon we are at table eating a love-meal like the one of three weeks earlier when the brain-scan result brought them— Maartje, Paul (Jack's eldest brother), Hans, Raewyn. Now it is just the three of us, Jack, Maartje and me, and we all eat up like good little boy and girls.

Then suddenly I am moved to do what I have never done at table before. Yes ... I will do it. I will read from scripture in true Presbyterian style and then I will say a little prayer. Perhaps I chose words about the resurrection from Saint John or Saint Paul, I don't know. The sequence that took palce completely overshadowed my endeavor, *itself* becoming the reading and the prayer.

Jack's eyes are fixed on my face, drawing mine to his own, and all at once I must look up at him without knowing why. I turn cold—has his face really changed so alarmingly? I don't know this face .... God. I want him to die soon. Please, please God. *Soon*. Don't let anything happen to his eyes—I'm so afraid for him.

Please let his eyes always be beautiful. (I told the radiotherapist about my fear and he assured me death would come first, come long before my dread was realized, but the waiting for the release of death is now even more difficult to bear than the thought of life without him.) As we look at each other, expressing the inexpressible, there is no trace of fear in his eyes, only a plea.

To my surprise I hear my own voice speaking, uttering words I haven't thought till the moment I am compelled to say them. My darling, I surrender you to the Lord if that is what he wants. Jack gives me a little half smile—or is that just the way his mouth is now? There is love in his eyes, and relief. This very night the Lord's call comes and Jack begins his most momentous journey. A going into God.

If only I could say, Wait for me . . . . But on this solo inward journey into the unknown there is no provision for company, no heartwarming legend to soften the reality and conquer death by love like Savitri.[1]

Yet Love *has* conquered death, and by a reality even harsher than death itself. His light will be a lamp to Jack's feet and his arms will be outstretched in welcome: Come, you whom my Father has blessed, take for your heritage the kingdom prepared for you since the foundation of the world.

The river of life, alive with all the meanings of both of us and all the lives infusing ours, will bear him from me finally but oh, to what a destiny . . . the boundless sea of knowledge where

> Unto the furthest flood-brim look
>   with me
> Still, leagues beyond those leagues
>   there is more sea[2]

—humanity's cumulative striving for completion, then God himself, and Truth in all its infinitude where to know is still not to know and the known remains mystery.

The following morning when I told our priest about my offering of Jack, he said: Shirley, *that* was the true healing. It was *you* who were healed.

_____

How grateful I was for that last fortnight at home. he has been eating and sleeping well, without headaches, without nausea, thanks to the miracle drug which gives him a sense of well-being. The four-hourly painkillers too have done their work but at night only one has been enough to carry him through—in itself a little miracle. That is why I was deceived ... thinking only of the restoration of his physcial health, his material body. Despite all my faith I was in Plato's cave, nursing illusions.

But not any more. I have been healed of my nonacceptance. I have let him go. Our priest had a better understanding of things and in his prayer with us in our living room at the time he received Jack into the church, he thanked God for the wisdom and foresight with which he had made me part of Jack's life so that Jack would not be alone at the end.

Now as I look back I can only thank God too that similar provision has been made for me, though in a different way. In letting me encounter with Jack the solitude of death, all my fear of it has been taken away, simply transformed into wonder and longing and tender, tender dread. Darwin once observed of the lonely places of the earth in South America: "No one can stand in those solitudes unmoved and not feel that there is more in man than the breath of his body." How much more would this be true of witnessing the actual moment of change from the state of impermanence to that which endures?

Now that I have surrendered Jack I realize how hard it has been for him, poor darling, tired as he was, to keep on trying for my sake to get well. Tonight, because I have released him, he will soon be on his way—and he wants to go. Deep in my soul I feel the peace of this, far below the deadly pain, and the privilege it is to be near him as he goes without reluctance or fear toward the rolling blue at the desert's edge.

After this things begin to happen fast and at midnight my senses electrify into alertness as I hear the rush of feet and spring out of bed quickly to follow Jack to the bathroom. He is vomiting (the two-week reprieve over), and suddenly he cannot move. The paralysis has come ... finally ... just as the radiotherapist said it would.

Fortunately the district nurse arrives without delay and she takes over gently and capably, inching his crippled body down the passageway. Maartje and I fall away helplessly. He manages to speak to her despite the tautness of his face

muscles, and she manages to understand despite the distortion of his
speech. I will always bless her for understanding. Will I be able to stay here for a
little while? 'he asks. Yes, she reassures
him soothingly. But I don't want to be a
burden to Shirley.

Unconsciously Jack has expressed a
universal fear of the terminally ill: fear of
separation from familiar scenes and beloved faces; fear of helplessness and the
strain on loved ones. But for him, thank
God, there will be no more hospitals.
His own bed and my loving arms will
be his vehicle to perpetual peace.

The nurse gets him back into bed,
easing him in with great care and dexter-
ous gentleness. He can still move his
right hand and he clasps mine tightly,
scratching my palm, very hard, three
times. I didn't understand till two days
later he was saying I-love-you.

My precious love ... Why didn't I
bend down and kiss you ...? Why didn't
I put my arms around you ...? Cry
over you ...? Why am I so numb and
underreacting, functioning only like an
automaton ...?

Tomorrow the nurse will tell me what you said and I will be so comforted. Your last spoken thought was of me, your last word my name.

But it is already tomorrow: the day, Friday, October 6; the time, the border hour between night and morning when all sounds, city and country, are at a minimum. Sleep yawns itself to rest or stretches itself awake, or simply continues its deep restoring work. The nurse says nothing further can be done and prepares to leave after providing me with all that is needed. Shall I call the doctor? I want to know. In the morning, she answers.

The vomiting continues at intervals and the bleakest vigil of my life begins, though bleak only in an earthly sense. There is no Prophet Elisha to comfort me with the words: Have no fear, there are more on our side than on theirs.... Or to pray over me: Lord open her eyes and make her see.... But I know I am loving Jack right into heaven and the old Shirley is dying too.

Every moment I want to call the doctor but every moment I hold back, something Maartje cannot understand, neither for that matter can I. Only afterwards, when I am torn apart by my failure, does the answer come to me, setting my tormented mind at rest and giving me a new theme for praise. Unpracticed as I was in this unrehearsed and fundamental role of ministering to the dying, the grace of the occasion supplied all my need though it did not spare me the trauma of indecision.

Each time Jack needs it I support his head, now a leaden weight because the buoyancy of life has gone—dear God, don't let it drop backward and choke him. Please darling ... please, *please*.

His legs too are like dead weights as I try to lift them. Even if I had wanted to ease his position by turning him every few hours I would not have been able to do it. I pray he didn't feel the cramp from the paralysis or the nine long hours of waiting for release once he had lapsed into a coma at about five in the morning. His last action before he becomes semiconscious takes me completely by surprise: with a determined terrible effort he straightens his folded arms and throws off his covering.

My God, what shall I do? is my uncertain, frightened response. The early morning air is biting, even if I close the window. Shall I cover him again or let him become chilled? I cover him again, lightly; just the blankets, not the quilt. (Thank God Maartje is there to prompt me.) Forgive me if this adds to your fiery ordeal, but my ordeal is more fiery and it will last much longer. Every decision involves me in later turmoil for not having done the opposite—such is the oversolicitude of love. Meanwhile time petrifies in a crisis, every second in the minute creeping along riveted backward: hours, days, years, eternity.

Jack's candle is burning before a picture of the Blessed Mother and Child in our bedroom and she at least is praying to her Son—I could never doubt that—making up for all that is wanting in me. I don't need to tell her how I feel. She has been there—on Calvary. This is not just a man, any man, who is dying. This is *Jack*. Someone who has spoken praise to her in Gabriel's words and in her own words to Elizabeth.... I know we are not walking alone. She has met us on the way as she met Jesus straining along the endless road of his cross. Pray for us sinners now, and at the hour of our death. She hasn't forgotten.

The sun energizes, the winds disperse seeds, the rain brings life. We don't need to know how or why it happens, only to be grateful *that* it happens.

At about five o'clock in the morning I call the doctor. Hello, Jack, he says. I am going to give you an antinausea injection. Jack reacts almost immediately, one of his pupils dilating so that the iris practically disappears. He is unconscious, the doctor interprets. Is he in pain? (Please God, don't let there be any pain.) No, he feels nothing, the doctor assures me.

Raewyn is the first to arrive, pale, heartbroken. She is 21 and Jack is the only father she has ever known since the age of four when he married a divorcee and took her in with two of her brothers. No child of his own body could have been a better daughter to him and, though I don't know it yet, she is to be his greatest bequest to me. Believing he knows all that is going on I tell him: Darling, Raewyn is here. And I place her hand in his.

While we wait around his bedside, emotionally drained and spiritually numb, I suggest to Maartje we sing songs of praise to help us pray and keep our thoughts directed as Nature labors to bring Jack to his birth among the unfathomable marvels of the Lord.

Be still and know that I am God
Be still and know that I am God
Be still and know that I am God

I am the Lord that healeth thee
I am the Lord that healeth thee
I am the Lord that healeth thee

In thee O Lord do I put my trust
In thee O Lord do I put my trust
In thee O Lord do I put my trust

Somehow we force our voices not to break. At least my lips are uttering the offering I am trying to make—the surrender of my love.

Thou art worthy, thou art worthy
Thou art worthy O Lord
To receive glory, glory and honor
Glory and honor and power
For thou hast created
Hast all things created
Thou hast created all things
And for thy pleasure they are created
Thou art worthy O Lord

At a quarter to six I call our priest. He has to offer the early Mass but will come straight after. And he then telephones the prayer group that Jack is dying. Next I call Gay and Norman.

Jack is lying still like one in a deep restful sleep, his breathing unlabored and steady—no, there can't be any pain. Could there be dreams . . .? Insignificant little dreams of him, Norm and Jim over their pint in those last days when he couldn't go to the pub any more, or ever again, and I invited them here every

Thursday, "their" day? The three of them ... extracting humor to the nth degree from everything conceivable!

I envy you being the fly on the wall, Gay laughs over the telephone. Oh, I keep well out of sight—don't want to spoil their fun! Do you know or can you ever know what it has cost me to love you? No, you will just go your way to bliss and forget me and leave me to the unloving of you—if only I could.

Though we feel no joy, Maartje and I try to sing Mary's triumphant and glorious words of praise.

My soul doth magnify the Lord
My soul doth magnify the Lord
And my spirit hath rejoiced in God
    my Savior
For he that is mighty hath done
    great things
And holy is his name

Presently Gay and Norman arrive in stricken silence and as I open the door to them Gay begins to upset herself but I calm her down. All their concern for us is in her eyes, all the telephone calls she has made and received to and from various friends, all the help in the garden, all the little messages sent to Jack to give his spirits a lift. Once more I tell him who his visitors are and then I place his hand in theirs. Soon they are gone and at last our priest arrives.

He stands silently beside Jack looking down at him. Jack ... let go, he says almost prayerfully. Don't worry about Shirley. Then: Shirley, come here. Stand in front of his eyes. He is looking at you.

O my God, this is my inadequate moment—I cannot return Jack's look. Rather, I look, but my eyes say nothing. Is this what you see, my darling, a mask standing before you? Your unblinking gaze is insupportable.... Suppose your eyelids are immobile, your eyes drying out like shrinking pools? The thought is too much for me. There ... that will ease the burning. You understand, don't you, why I closed your eyes.

The battery of my inundating persecuting thoughts comes later, comes relentlessly. *Why* did I do this? Eyes are only closed at death, not before, and I shut out the little that was left of Jack's world—I have lost forever what his eyes were telling me. O God, why am I so *insensitive*?

No one is in the room at this moment but the priest and I standing side by side, our eyes on Jack. He puts his arm around me, awkwardly but firmly, intending to convey by gesture what words alone could not express. Shirley, I am far more worried about *you* than I am about Jack, he says. I mumble something. Words with no meaning. But I am greatly touched. Never before have I felt so close to the outreaching compassion of Jesus.

We now call the others in and Father begins the prayers for the dying.

Go forth from this world, O Christian soul, in the name of God the Father almighty who created you, in the name of Jesus Christ, the Son of the living God, who suffered for you, in the name of the Holy Spirit who has been poured upon you. . . . May peace be your dwelling today, and may your home be in holy Sion.

Amen, we answer. Let it so be.

Time hangs like a dead pendulum with all of us in limbo waiting for the inevitable to happen, and throughout the day people pour in to spend a little time with Jack. His breathing is still regular but he is deep in relative death, beyond the point of human recall. Only afterwards will it strike me as extraordinary that in spite of the earlier vomiting and later incontinence the sheets remained as fresh as when I had made up the bed. I can never be grateful enough that Jack was spared becoming a burden to himself and others as he so feared.

It is long past midday now and Jack's candle has burned itself out. My darling, it is not easy to die. Our last visitor is a priest and he invites me to pray with him. We kneel together by the bedside and each of us prays aloud, my prayer stilted and cold ... words, random words ... fit only for the "junkyard of heaven."

I can't help feeling the Lord accepts

the priest's prayer, not mine, as the final one. (Six years later this feeling was put to rights when an old man I knew who had been in a coma for five days in a hospice died immediately after my visit and prayer for his release.)

Slowly Jack is coming to the border of that purified world where the ills and evils of the human heart no longer have a place. Time will accelerate as it surges to meet the timeless, gathering him in its two arms of past and future against its bosom of the present and sweeping him along on a vast current of loving energy to his true place in the Light.

Somewhere in that limitless embrace there will be room for both of us and we will find each other again ... will find our love again ... will find our friends again ... and all the happiness denied to us on earth, and the knowledge and love beyond our understanding here.

My tears are not for Jack without Shirley, but for Shirley without Jack. He will be open to the *spheres*—the *waters*—the *spirit*. He will stand at the heart of unrevealed eternity. And when saturated in the radiance of that knowing, will he see me too with different eyes, not as I am but as I want to be? And when I come, will there be anything left for us to see together, once he has seen it all?

How graciously our God respects our sense of time.... Shirley, another friend will say, the Lord didn't take Jack until you let him go. Straight into the sunlight like an ecstatic skylark dizzy with song and dance, straight into the sunlight you go, freed from your nest by the need to fly into the rapturous unending heavens which are the everlasting arms surrounding and upholding you.

It is now 2:30 p.m. and for the first time today I am alone with my Jack. I look at him uncertain what to do. Is this pitiful helpless heap all that remains of him—my husband?

These hands ... they were so strong once. Both of mine would have fit into one of his. How he loved me to trim his nails, lazybones that he was, and how he always staged a great pantomime about not trusting me until *once* I justified his big fuss and accidentally gave him a wee little nick! My darling My darling.

Suddenly I am moved to lie down beside him, close, acting out a silent inspiration as if the part has been given to me. He is turned to the left, and I enfold him with my right arm. Words come to my lips that I have so often spoken before. I love you, my darling. Bending over him I kiss his ear gently again and again.

If all the marvels of the world were handed to me on a wonder-heaped plate encrusted with the moons of Jupiter and rimmed by the rings of Saturn to annihilate my consciousness, they would fall far short of the sublime miracle that now happens within the circle of my arms. He starts to go blue, beginning at his right ear where I have kissed him. My arm is still wrapped around him, cradling him. Like the morning star melting into the sun he slips away without a struggle ... just one last small breath like a delicate sigh and he has given up his body.

Maartje! I cry out loudly. Maartje, *he's gone*. She comes running in and we clasp each other tightly and cry, letting go completely till the room resounds with the sound of our sobs. But there is exaltation in my tears and blessed blessed release.

He knew. He was waiting *for me* to set his spirit free. All this time he was waiting for my personal farewell, my final words of love that would live in his memory forever and be a part of his soaring joy. He didn't go before our leave-taking was done.

This is a moment so intense and glorious that it blots out from the cosmic canvas every lesser or unworthy moment I have imprinted on it during the course of our short relationship. In the long dark months of depression ahead of me when the whole creation will lose its brightness and even a crane could not pick me up and restore me to joy, *this* moment will rise like a brilliant undiscovered star flooding me with its hidden light and reminding me that God *is* LOVE, and Jack still IS. Death has branded our love into LIFE forever. Through these long years of silence and waiting it will bond us forever unseparated in God's love. And could it ever be that he would not be there to welcome me with joy when I have farewelled him in such pain?

The angry times in which I said with childish venom "I hate you" are now canceled by my last affirmation of love. When memory becomes a remorseless tyrant, I must not forget this last out-pouring of the precious spikenard. One day I will be as grateful for the angry times as for the loving ones, when I can think again without anguish of the lost little look on his face because he didn't know what subtle, elusive annoyances were getting at me—and I didn't know either! But always: I'm sorry, darling. And always the goodnight prayer to-gether. Always the I love you which was the I hate you in disguise.

Lord, you are the true interpreter. You know the why and what of each of us, and our mistakes aren't poured in concrete—irreversible—but in your blood, washed out everlastingly. You gave him to me in love, and in love I have given him back to you.

I thought he was mine, but he wasn't.

I hoped he would live, but he didn't.

Yet Jack is not just dead forever, he is healed and whole forever.

Being flows towards him like a boundless stream of things, meanings, persons and happenings....

... Death is, therefore, by reason of
its very being, the moment above
all others for the awakening of
consciousness....

God himself stretches out His hand
for him; God who, in every stirring of
his existence, had been in him as his
deepest mystery....[3]

I do not need to hold him tightly any
more to shut out the words of doom.

The day was also a Friday, September
15, Feast of Our Lady of Sorrows. The
doctor had come to tell us the result of
the brain-scan. You've brought good
news, I smiled at him, confident to the
last. No, the news is very bad ... I
want you both to come in and sit down
(we were outside working on a pebble
garden). But we are grateful for the
truth.

Now the eyes I closed will never close
again.

They are sunlight on this broken column.

NOTES

1   In ancient Hindu legend, Savitri—unlike Orpheus in the Greek—saved her husband Satyavan from the world of the dead.
2   From one of Dante G. Rossetti's sonnets entitled "The Choice."
3   Ladislaus Boros: *The Mystery of Death* (New York: Crossroads, 1973).

Part Two

Now ... The Learning and Remembering

... all the pains and deaths of the
    world
Shall be mother-pains in the birth
    of life
... all the dancing lovely leaves
Which whisper forever
That life is forever,
A going and a going
Into the night of light.
Patrick Mooney—
Death and Resurrection

3

"That's Jack"

Time mine enemy
that will not in passing
appease pain.
The same hour repeated
brings yesterday's grief,
the swelling moment's expectation
made void again.
In the courageous hour
the heart hides
in the strength that faith bestows.
But oh my loneliness,
ancient as Eden's desolation
when Adam was alone.
Now, the role reversed,
Eve living
dies of her sorrow.

Amiti Grech—Widow[1]

AS the heavy months closed in around me I realized how little I really knew of the sensitive, proud, reserved man who had been my husband for the space and time of two and a half years. I now had a great longing to know something about the part of Jack's life I had not shared, so I wrote to his family in Holland, in Britain, and here in New Zealand for their memories of those early years.

Slowly a picture emerged. He went to a special school because of learning difficulties ... had a good relationship with his teacher ... was happy in himself and loved by everybody ... grew up normal, practical, very honest, very shy and quiet ... became a member of the Y.M.C.A. ... loved poetry ... was clever with his hands....

But the great romance of his life was art—and here is where I get a lump in my throat. This sensitive, artistic person who spent most of his free time in museums, churches and other monumentalized buildings, and who bought art books with the little money he had, had no chance to develop his talent. The

War took care of that. If he had not been born 25 years too early, his sister Maske wrote from England, he would have had that chance. This faintly echoes something I have read . . . Vincent van Gogh . . . for him recognition came 25 years too late.

The War came and went, one of history's unspeakables. Jack's parents had the money but 10 children made food a constant and desperate source of anxiety—there simply wasn't any to buy. Paul remembers *walking* to the other side of Holland (about 144 kilometers) to get a bag of potatoes! The German Army requisitioned the local school and that ended Jack's primary education and even ruled out secondary because he was ready for work by the time the occupation was over five years later. So the artist in him remained untrained and unexpressed.

I could not even imagine what he looked like as a little boy and as a young man, and when his sister Pieta sent me some old photos from Holland it was too much for me. In place of the hair that I knew, shining like black silver and very smooth and fine in texture and as profuse as a young man's, is this unfamiliar sweep, this dandy puff I do not know.... But I recognize the imposing, compelling brows that give his eyes so much depth and distance. How subtly he could use them too.... And the face that I knew and still know because I will never forget it, had some lines of wear and tear and vivid black sideburns, so much a part of his handsomeness....

His build was always very slight, and I suppose his philosophy of moderation had a lot to do with it. He never ate or drank too much. He believed that when you left the table you should have enough room left to be able to eat the same amount over again—his father's maxim, I think it was.

Jack spoke very little about his childhood, in fact there were only three incidents he sketchily shared between sips of sherry or mouthfuls of beer, like the tiny delicate strokes of an artist's brush, that allowed me just a glimpse or two of him as a little boy. There was one rather hurt little memory that stood out like a dike, the day his mother accused him of stealing cookies out of a jar when one of his brothers "done it." The matter was never resolved. And, as if to balance it, a reminiscence of a happier nature concerning Hans, his younger brother by 18 months.

It was Hans' birthday and their mother was at her wit's end trying to dream up some combination of witchery and hardship that could possibly interest and excite a child. Meanwhile Hans' expectations were running very low—who would remember it anyway? And wouldn't Happy Birthday in wartime have a hollow ring?

Mothers are ingenious people however, and they never admit defeat. Before Hans' wonder-struck eyes there suddenly appeared a vision of the most unutterable, ravishing delight . . . an old coffeepot burnished to red-gold and crammed with lollies!

Hans went high on the originality and unexpectedness of it and to him it obviously had the impact of a birthday party with all the trimmings. No other present before or since, Jack maintained, had ever brought so much pleasure to Hans, and from the number of times he alluded to it in that special conspiratorial undertone that signifies a communication, it was clear that the old resurrected coffeepot had immortalized itself in both boys' minds.

Then, as the War tapered off, there was the vivid recollection of the day the Red Cross came to Alphen on the Rhine (Jack's hometown) distributing bread, butter and sugar rations to every individual there—people who had nearly forgotten what these basic food items tasted like.

In their early 20s Jack and Hans left their nest in the west Netherlands (Alphen is about 24 kilometers from Amsterdam and halfway to The Hague), said goodbye to the great museums and glorious churches of Europe, steeled their hearts to take leave of parents, family and country, and came to New "Zeeland" to start a new life. Maartje, Paul and their families were already here.

They arrived in Wellington and came on to Napier where Jack got his first job as a painter for a contractor and was launched on a series of confrontations with the intricacies of the English language! Then, after many moves which included the South Island and much water under the bridge, Jack came full circle: Napier again, and me. But time is something we were not given, or rather, the little we were given was enough to draw to ourselves all it was meant to give.

Altogether Jack was in New Zealand nearly 27 years and he was completely a New Zealander at heart. Do you want to come back to Holland to live? his family eagerly wanted to know when we visited them a year after our marriage. Though I am sure he was torn, he managed a gentle but emphatic *no*, tempering it with a big smile. Despite two trips back he had grown away from it and only his family and his love for the great Dutch masters linked him with the old country.

Has he now met them all face to face, the old masters—Rembrandt, Frans Hals, Albrecht Dürer, El Greco, Titian, Caravaggio, Giotto, Van Eyck? And his other favorites too—Cézanne, Van Gogh, Gauguin, Renoir, Picasso? Has he said hello to my favorites: Vermeer, Chagall and Escher?

Perhaps, without probing, certain secrets have been revealed to him, secrets of the devastating commitment of the great masters often in the face of poverty, tragedy and rejection. Yet for him the price was not high enough and though in another and better world he may write his name like theirs in paint, in this one he must be content that I will write it in humble print.

I remember how both of us stood enraptured before Constable in the London Art Gallery and how after the uninspiring reproductions I had been accustomed to seeing that had left me cold I was now gazing hypnotized at the glory of transfigured canvas wondering how it could possibly have erupted in all that *beauty*.

What did I tell you, darling! Jack's voice was triumphant. There is no comparison between an original and a print. No indeed, there isn't. The original is *alive*—O my God. What good is an alive original when Jack is dead? Please . . . let me just plod on.

Vermeer. Oh, the revelation! We are in the Mauritshuis Museum in The Hague and I am standing before Vermeer's *Head of a Girl*, prickling all over, rapt, unbelieving—could she be the faery princess of the poet Keats' enchanted world? Her flesh is soft and glowing, her eyes exquisitely tender, and the blue of her scarf so pure that no reproduction has captured it.

When we are home again and I take another look at the print of the same subject hanging in our living room, I am filled with sorrow at the injustice done to the creators of such masterpieces to bring their work into our humble, unworthy abodes. There should be a law against this mass reproduction. Once in a lifetime one should make the pilgrimage.

Jack made that pilgrimage daily in his mind as he worshiped at the shrine of art, never seeming to get tired of reading about it . . . all that homework. I took a shortcut and simply picked his brains. And he didn't mind, poor darling. He even allowed me to outtalk him sometimes on his pet subject.

That is a Matisse, he said admiringly while contemplating a gaudy print in a host's dining room. Oh really? *I* thought it had been splashed together by one of the children! He could look at a painting and immediately place it with hardly ever a mistake . . . could talk about any period in the history of art, the tensions and setbacks that had converted to power in execution, in enigmatic color, in bizarre themes, in wildly beautiful or imaginative or provocative or disturbing or simply serene creations.

I say it all with pride and also with sorrow because he so keenly felt the frustration of love and longing that were handicapped by lack of developed talent.

In a letter to his friend Émile Bernard, Van Gogh expresses his ideas of further development after death "assuming that in the innumerable other planets and suns, lines, shapes and colors also exist, we may keep a comparatively open mind about the possibilities of painting on a higher, different level of existence." Later in the same letter he says:

At one time the earth was supposed to

be flat. Well, so it is, even today, from Paris to Asnieres. But that fact doesn't prevent science from proving that the earth as a whole is spherical. . . . In spite of that, we are still at the stage of believing that life itself is flat, the distance from birth to death. Yet the probability is that life, too, is spherical and much more extensive and capacious than the hemisphere we know at present.

My own thought in its shabby rags has suddenly been given an eye-catching new gown, a cynosure, intoxicating in the perspective it suggests, like the limitless new worlds that open up with each new magnification. Yet even the most outreaching imagination will fail when it comes to the reality: Things no eye has seen, no ear has heard, no human heart conceived, the welcome God has prepared for those who love him.

I know there will be nothing wanting for my loved one in his Father's house: My son, all that I have is yours. Art so vast and dazzlingly extravagant that he will have to be given a new perception to be able to enjoy it. No more frustration. No more longing. Only the heaven of the Absolute in whom there is no need.

And I, who am neither an artist nor a poet, must somehow catch the flavor of him and make him live in this little book as he does in my heart. But it isn't only in our hearts that our dear ones live.

Is it possible there could be records and traces everywhere of life on this planet in all their mind-blowing variations—skeletons of the "Little People," live frogs in marble, fishes in tree gum, metamorphoses of every description in plant, animal and stone— yet no trace of our dear ones and all that they are, as opposed to what they have achieved and left behind, because they have gone from view? Wiped out as if they had never been?

I would find *that* more difficult to believe than the most far-fetched theory of life beyond the grave. I think Van Gogh wrote more truly than he realized when he raised the eternal question as to whether we can see the whole of life or only know a hemisphere of it before death, and put forward the idea that "cholera, the stone, tuberculosis and cancer are all celestial modes of locomotion like ships, buses and trains here below while if we die peacefully of old age we make the journey to the stars on foot" (Letter to his brother Theo). At any rate, his despairing yet hope-filled words "There is an art in the future, and it will be so beautiful, so young!" seem to have a meaning beyond our present earthly existence.

I remember the day, shortly after the funeral, when I forced myself to go into Jack's studio-den behind the garage. Why is a car so much identified with the person who drove it? And as if that weren't enough, here are his garden shoes . . . still mud-caked. If he is anywhere in memory, he is here.

As I enter this special place I read the message of protecting love, for he has set it all up like a last will and testament, giving me the most perfect expression of himself. An art book is open on the table—if only I had noted the page. The little manikin on the shelf is poised like a ballet dancer in midperformance. The paints lie open. His paintings, done in

Warren's class, are stacked against the wall. The room is empty, yet full. But epitomizing the whole scene, welcoming me the moment I enter, is his favorite canvas on the easel looking down at me. He was always proud of it because Warren had singled it out as the best of ten for its discipline and its dedication to the principles of art which he was trying to teach at night school.

Now, louder than words, this painting is speaking to me. It is his bequest to me. And if beauty lies in the eyes of the beholder, there is nothing more dazzling in the entire Renaissance than this. I have photographed it, in fact, all of them, the one he did in the style of Monet, and the others, though incomplete, to be able to take them with me wherever I go, symbols of hope, of the best yet to be, in a future beyond deprivation where the cup overflows. Hope is love waiting, our priest once said.

Jack . . . Art . . . Holland. . . .

How much I wanted to show him India too. India, and her "sunset stones of glory," her "marble halls of fame," her philosophical greatness and limitless variety. To me they are all forever un-separated and I want to take the whole of it in my arms and hold it and hold it.

Some need to drain the cup before they can taste the wine. For me this one little sip from the brimming cup of eternity will surfeit me to the end of my days while I wait in expectant faith for the "life of the world to come" in which I say every Sunday: *I believe*.

From now on I can only tell you about the Jack *I* knew.

If I were asked to write my impressions of the first few days of experiencing loss till after the funeral, I think there would be two thoughts uppermost in my mind. First, the way I personally was affected by what happened; and then, the almost miraculous way everything ran on oiled wheels thanks to the kindness and generosity and hard work of those caught up in the events, those who made their superb individual contributions so that the whole left nothing jarring, nothing that didn't seem an integral part of the story or wasn't completely uplifting and beautiful.

The weather gave our spirits a little symbolic lift as the heavy rain of the night before and the prevailing southerly did not deter the sun from putting in a courtesy appearance, plainly showing that even Nature smiles through her tears.

I was asked to provide something representing Jack to be carried up to the altar with the bread, water and wine for the Eucharist, and what better symbol could there have been than his candlestick whose light had burned at all the sacraments through which grace had been poured on him in the last ten days of his life. It had even lit him on his journey into perpetual light.

Truer than that candle flame was Jack's beautiful patience, already shining like a nearing star. During the entire time of his sickness there was not one complaint—he never once blamed God, or his work, or the doctors, or himself. Never once did he express regret about not being able to paint in his studio, about not living to enjoy his house, about losing the hopes of his future retirement (admittedly about 15 years away) and all the wonderful leisure he would use so creatively. All his plans have ended so abruptly and he has been cut off in his prime, but no ... there is no repining. He quietly accepts the unvarnished truth: the time has come to face his own mortality, to return to Mother Nature and Father God.

This is not stoicism, this is grace. Love works in countless ways, even through ostensibly "bad" ones. God can create out of a million wrong ways the one right way for a person at a given time as he did for the criminal who found it in a prison cell, and for the professional thief who stopped blaspheming and cursing his awful fate of crucifixion and found faith, hope and love at that eleventh hour because he heard words he had never heard before: Father, forgive them; they do not know what they are doing. God can even create, all-loving as he is, opportunities after death for a change of heart for those who are still teachable.

This is why our priest's choice of the

beatitudes for the gospel reading was and remains music to my heart, because, he said, *that's Jack*. Jack was not rich or famous. He had no great talents, no special achievements to leave to posterity. Yet the eightfold blessing was to be his for his detachment of spirit, his gentleness, his kindness, his cleanness of heart. He would be comforted after the long mourning and all his longings would find fulfillment.

Jack ... lively, human, irritating, wholly lovable, never causing psychological harm to anyone, never boring; the self-made man, self-educated, self-disciplined, slow to anger; laughing, gentle, unassuming. Jack peeling the potatoes for tea to ensure they would be on the menu; and infuriating me with his low-key, underreacting manner— the common male trait of habitually understating things!

Jack escorting me very proudly to Sunday Mass, even before we were married, sitting with his hands tucked away under his thighs, his face upturned, his eyes glued on the celebrant (How I love to watch him, he's so attentive, a well-wisher smiles); then at home often turning on the radio to the church service, either morning or evening, to feed his hunger for spiritual things. Jack tinkering around in the garage, puffing contentedly and listening to an afternoon concert; or gardening, reading, painting, watching television; or doing the dishes after tea; or fostering in me Bach, Mozart, Beethoven; or making his usual weather comment: It's not tropical.

Happy and blessed he was and is ! He who could be just as touchy as I, though granted on a ratio of one to a thousand! There was the time we went to the movies during our friendship days and his hand was placed very conspicuously on his knee, but I didn't jump to the bait. On the way home he was sulking furiously, and finally I wormed it out. I hadn't put my hand in his—and it was *waiting*! But, silly, why didn't *you* take *my* hand?

I had usually been content to let him take the initiative—how could I have known I was being put to the test and found hopelessly wanting! By and by I developed the habit, whenever we drove, of placing my arm across the top of his seat-back and cupping the nape of his neck in my hand. Then the day came when he would never get rid of my attentions. . . .

Jack, a saint as human as they come, the way God likes us because he made us and was human too. The casket glows in the reflected candlelight according to his last request, the cheapest available. . . . Soon the six concelebrating priests will stand around it and officially pray:

Saints of God, come to his aid
Come to meet him, angels of the
    Lord
Receive his soul and present him
    to God the Most High.

Our priest's homily was a triumph and all his homework was rewarded when the Dutch names tripped off his tongue: Martinus and Masje, the parents, then family overseas and here—no small achievement, considering Jack had three brothers and six sisters: Paul, Maartje, Bas, Pieta, Hans, Maske, Paulien, Bep and Hannie (Jack came between Pieta and Hans).

There were actually 11 children but one little boy had died in infancy and Jack who came after him had been given his name (in the same way as Vincent van Gogh had been named for the dead baby brother who preceded him—a Dutch custom perhaps?). I found it very strange that Jacobus Two should have been the first to follow Jacobus One. To the family Jack was known as Koos (sounded Kose) but he changed to Jack in New Zealand because his workmates started calling him Jim!

Then our priest comes to Jack and Shirley. But if, as in a Jewish funeral, his homily was intended to release tears, it failed completely for mine are a river and they are dammed by a pinhole. If sorrow could be shared its burden would be lightened but it is too extreme, demanding solitude—and the church is full.

We met in our middle years, he is saying.... Our backgrounds were widely differing yet our marriage was a great success.... Jack is healed and whole.... Our prayers for him have been fully answered....

In a remark to me later this discerning

man perfectly summed up our relationship: I have never seen a couple do so much for each other in such a short time. I am not sure in retrospect what I have done for Jack, but I know with piercing clarity what he has done for me. In some mysterious way he was Jesus for me because through his patience in suffering and through the pain of losing him I began to see myself as I had never seen myself before.

Perhaps without Jack the words *I love you* would not have meant what they mean now because the more one person suffers on account of the suffering of another, the greater the love that is born between them. Christmas, Calvary, the Bible, the Mass, they are all about the self-offering of God in love. . . . I didn't understand this at the time—in fact I don't think I ever will—as I walked up to the altar after the reading of the Word, having handed the bread and wine to Maartje and Jack's candlestick to Raewyn while I myself carried the water that would be mixed symbolically with the wine.

If *I* had not put in those nails myself,

Jesus never would have conquered me or made me think more tenderly toward the wounded heart of all humanity. But our priest took my offering first, and when he had accepted the others he gave Jack's candle to me to light from the candle burning beside the casket, then he took it from me and placed it on the altar. I was deeply moved by the delicacy of the gesture—I thought only God knew what it cost me not to carry up Jack's candlestick myself. But now it is doubly blest, for both Raewyn and I have offered it.

All the while I waited eagerly for the peace greeting after the Lord's Prayer so that God could change something I couldn't, something that rankled and hurt, and that I so much wanted to put right ... Hans. We had got off to a wrong start when Jack was courting me and there was little real affection between us.

As the priests came down from the altar platform to greet us I embraced each member of Jack's family, but I held Hans with special warmth. his peace be with you ... and you ... the peace of

Jesus. And I knew immediately the antagonism had been laid to rest.

This interior reconciliation which I look upon as the first fruits of Jack's death was further cemented when I distributed some of his personal possessions and gave Hans the special suit. Jack wore it with so much love, I told him. With the same love I am giving it to you.

Only someone who has been through it would know the immense distance between you and all the people around you as the body of your loved one is slowly carried out of the church. They see only the wooden box and you a whole indefinable lifetime. He is really buried in your heart, and this they can never see. Outside I was caught up in a surge of grateful thank-you's but I could have been standing on an almost vertical incline with reality slipping, slipping away. . . .

Our priest rescued me with the down-to-earth reminder that he had another engagement at twelve and we must move on to the cemetery. With the next step mapped out for me I felt a little more secure. There can be nothing more dismaying than being in the public eye when you want to be out of sight even of yourself and of life. Yet these kind people were friends and well wishers who were here to honor Jack's memory and to express sympathy for my loss.

At the gravesite the funeral director handed me a little spade filled with earth ... filled with all humanity ever rising from and ever consigned to *dust and ashes* ... filled with all our sinfulness and vulnerability and smallness. But the Lord has a father's pity; does he not know the stuff of which we are made, can he forget that we are dust?

My sad little clods of earth looked so insignificant in my hand. Remember, man, that you are dust, and into dust you will return. I couldn't empty them into the gaping hole without some loving words to soften the harshness of that terrible moment. I love you, my darling. I love you. How small and thin my voice sounds in this large empty place.

The funeral was a glorious occasion

that carried me on the crest of a caring church community and I was still in the euphoric state of shock. But now that eight long months of uncertainty had been finally laid to rest, and the friends, relations and prayer supporters had gone, and sympathizers had paid their courtesy condolence visits all in a lump, the truth began to confront me in its bleak totality. The enormity of it came slowly home to me: Jack had gone and would never come back. Our earthly life together was finished.

Perhaps this state is what is known as heartbreak, something akin to the dark obscurity of faith that cannot be filmed, taped, analyzed, subjected to repeatable experiments, and so is out of bounds to science but without which the glory is departed and everything is flat, one-dimensional, devoid of the aura of infinite possibility. Perhaps this is G-O-D in the secret shrine of my inmost being, taking me a step further than ardent belief, as natural as breathing, to whom my happiness in the forever-after is even more important than my happiness in the here-and-now.

The next two days were like some ineffectual anticlimax in an unreal play. Shirley, you are drained, our priest said gently. My mind dissociated itself from everything around me, even my most intimate self. In this fictional world the simplest action like making a cup of tea became unreal. We talked, gesticulated, smiled as usual, but nothing was the same anymore. I was part of a detached dream sequence taking place on another level of awareness. Grief is a drug and I was on a dislocating "trip."

However much I might have felt estranged and distanced from what was happening, sooner or later my changed awareness would have to come to grips with reality—the sooner the better. Would I ever be able to bounce back to normal? Feel again, sleep again, above all laugh again? Would I ever be able to want to eat again without having to force food down because reason dictated it?

Yes, I would. Now there might seem to be a deep dichotomy between mind and body, each acting under protest against the needs and functions of the other, but the plain truth is we can and do survive grief. A stark reality, very difficult to accept.

One of my reactions at the time of Jack's death was purely instinctive and I regret that my conditioning did not equip me to deal with it better. I sent his body away almost immediately ... without looking at it ... without touching it. When a dear friend came in and I un-covered it, her tears splashed down all over him—hers, instead of mine. But my eyes and my mind were closed against his body so I wasn't moved when I uncovered it. The tears I had briefly shed were for the spirit that had gone, not for the temple that had been vacated.

Later I would be filled with remorse for my unfeelingness but then I was too numb to feel. When all your emotions and sensibilities have been caught up in the protracted sadness and stretched almost to breaking, it takes a long while to wind down again and slip back to normal; somewhat like a mother slowly recovering her shape after a pregnancy. Knowing that death will eventually come does not diminish the shock when it actually does.

And just as well too because this aura of numbness surrounding you is really your best friend and without it you couldn't cope. It allows you to feel the emptiness all around you, his place at table, his pillow in bed, his pitiful slippers, but it cushions you so that you feel so much only, no more. Gradually you can adjust in your own way and grieve at your own pace. The surrounding darkness absorbs the acuteness of reality. Unbelievable as it may seem, Jack's photograph on the mantelpiece later triggered more tears, when I had the courage to look at it, than his body did after his death.

Also I then had privacy whereas with Jack lying dead in the house, the people around me, all a necessary part of the scene who arrived within minutes, blocked off my normal responses and left me artificially controlled. If some of them had put their arms around me and tried to comfort me I might have been able to cry—and God knows how great was my need of being comforted. But there would be time enough for tears in the crushing, empty, endless progression of unhurrying hours in front of me. *Then* I would be able to C-R-Y.

The numbness also helped me to think clearly and act decisively. I remember thinking when I saw in print the notice I had dictated for the papers, how ridiculous it was that an unwanted comma should niggle me so much at a time like this. And why hadn't I checked the punctuation?

And when it came to deciding where Jack's body had to lie in repose there was not a moment's hesitation. Raewyn was surprised that I wanted it to lie in the church, but this house was not his home any more and I couldn't have his body back here again. I knew Jack would be pleased about the church ... he loved Saint Mary's. It isn't dazzling or moving or historical like the churches in Britain and Europe, but no matter where we worshiped, either here or overseas, he always expressed his preference for that particular building and assembly, I suppose because he felt so at home there.

But darling, what about your *own* church? I used to ask, genuinely concerned about the monopolistic role of

mine and his consistently being a prac-
ticing non-Catholic Catholic! I'll go with
you to Saint Columba's (Presbyterian)—
I'd like to. Oh . . . (his whole face one
big smile) I couldn't be bothered going
to TWO services!

So now his body would repose in the
church he had made his own.

Of all the helps and graces that were
given to me at this very draining time the
vigil would have to receive special mention for immense security in the future,
and there were two ways in which it
helped to strengthen and stabilize me.
For those who do not know, the vigil
service in the Catholic church is a time of
special watching and prayer the evening
before a funeral or any important feast,
and that service really taught me the
value of a vigil.

We arranged that the vigil would be
on Sunday evening, the funeral on Mon-
day morning. Meanwhile Jack's family
(the New Zealand branch) had made the
long trip to Napier by car for the third
time. Immediately after our vigil service

a Holy Name service began, conducted by another priest, but I sat on in the church determined to stay all night. More than anything I needed to be alone ... before the Blessed Sacrament ... beside the casket ... and I was *going to stay*.

Paul and the family were against it, so was our priest, but they used very gentle persuasion. All right, Paul, you can come for me at ten o'clock. What time did that give me—this Holy Name service was interminable. (Please, Lord, take all these people away and give me some time alone with Jack. I have to tell him something. Surely you understand?)

As grateful as I was for the prayers of those around me I was happy to see the church slowly emptying because my unshed tears were pressing like a subterranean torrent against my temples and to be alone had become the most desirable of all desirable things, and also the most unattainable. Any personal prayer was out of the question until I was absolutely alone with the casket.

That miracle of solitude happened for the space of 30 minutes exactly; then several people came back in their great generosity, their kindness surrounding both Jack and me like the muted incandescence of the sanctuary lamp. But at least now I was alone, and gradually I became less tense. Gradually I was able to speak the terrible burden in my heart.

I looked round. It was safe now to let my sobs be heard by my ears alone. Darling ...

Darling, I let you suffer all those hours ... I didn't call the doctor, darling.... God ... I can't bear it, darling ... I can't ... *O God*. Why didn't I call the doctor ...? God ... why didn't I call him? Why did I let you *suffer*, darling?

Maartje kept telling me and I didn't listen. I didn't want to disturb him, or his pregnant wife, or his children. But I didn't care about *you* ... I failed you. I thought of everyone but you. I've not only killed you but I've let you die in agony. God, please let me die ... let me die *somehow* ... I can't make up for this any other way.

Then suddenly I stopped short in wonder—there was no mistaking Jack's voice, heard with my mind rather than my ears: *Darling, you did the right thing. What did the doctor do? He only gave me an injection to stop the vomiting. If I had had that injection with all that dinner inside me I wouldn't have been able to breathe easily and I would have suffered so much more. Because you didn't call him I got rid of it first.*

Don't you see darling, you helped me to be more comfortable. These words were imprinted on my consciousness in the sense that I knew instantaneously what Jack was "saying," and later the doctor's wife would tell me that I could have sent for him earlier but he would not have been able to do anything.

The relief poured into my soul as if the flood tide of peace had come, and I knew then how close Jack was. *Raewyn's name should be on the stone,* was the thought that came to me out of the blue as I stood looking down at his newly heaped grave, and I couldn't call the monument masons fast enough to tell them to add: AND DEARLY LOVED FATHER OF RAEWYN.

How often I have asked him to help me with this book and how often as a result the sentences flow. I have always believed in the friendship and love of the saints, God's loved and faithful children both human and angel, but this one was different ... this one was Saint Husband, a part of *me*.

By the time Paul came for me at ten, one aspect at least of my grief had been resolved making it easier for me to cope, just that little bit more, with whatever was to come. I do believe that if it were not for that wracked prayer of mine, I might not have been able to handle the terrible stress and turmoil to which I persisted in subjecting myself by going on and on with my bitter regrets and self-inflicted pain, claiming total responsibility that he whom I loved would still be here had not I, whom I felt I hated, so cruelly removed him.

That half hour of prayer in the silence of an empty church also contained a specific petition, and it was answered immediately, completely and permanently. I foresaw *fear*—all kinds of it—lurking in the shadows ready to take advantage of my helpless exposure to it, gloating over my aloneness in a big house with no children or pets to continue the sense of comfort and togetherness, maliciously waiting to prey on my imagination and overpower me with vague but real dread. But I forestalled it.

I prayed for the loving protection of the God who is also my parent, and I asked to be delivered from fear and all its inhibiting and diminishing ravages. After that my mind was so closed against it that there was no crack however small through which it could have entered. Simply by not admitting doubt and by refusing two offers of company during my first nights alone, I ensured that this spiritual programing took effect and worked powerfully.

I was set like a seal upon his heart, close as locket or bracelet fits and even my supreme fear of death evaporated into the earthlight of heaven.

This spiritual birth in which I had so travailed was the "breaking of the shell that enclosed my understanding." But if I, like Jack, am to shine at all it can only be in my own Shirley way, and the river I must cry on earth must be my passport to the lit-up immortal agape. From the depths I cry to you in the words of the singer of old:

In your good time, *answer* me.
In your *great love*, answer me.

NOTES

1   Amiti's very beautiful poem was given to me from a special manuscript of 105 of her poems.

4

**Like Fireflies
in the Night**

For even as love crowns you
so shall he crucify you.
Even as he is for your growth
so is he for your pruning.
      Kahlil Gibran—*The Prophet*

FIFTY golden years rounded out
by three extra months less one
day were Jack's allotted span.
On his birthday, July 7, I ordered a
special cake, perhaps the first of his life
that had ever carried his name, pale
primrose with white-lace icing and five
little candles each summarizing a dec-
ade. I invited his two closest friends
and their wives to dinner, along with

99

Raewyn and her husband. Then I brought out the infernal camera and took deceptive photographs in which we all smiled though our hearts were like cold stone.

There is no such thing as an age to die at or a time to die. Every time, theoretically, is the time to die, even before the drawing of the first breath or the taking of the first step. Where death is concerned age and health are both irrelevant, though no matter when it comes the time and manner of it are seldom acceptable.

But who are we to say when and where and how it should come, or why it shouldn't? And who are we to determine how time is apportioned to an individual life? The ancient Hindu and Chinese sages could only speculate; the Greeks were nearer because they understood through their great dramatists the power of suffering to exalt and redeem. What answer is there regarding the inscrutability of universal pain unless we look backward to the time on this planet when a beautiful young man sacrificed himself for an invisible kingdom?

He talked about great matters like life and death, love, forgiveness, and proper living, and the importance of the inner disposition over mere outward morality. It wasn't surprising that he made enemies in the oligarchic hierarchy of his day with all its jargon, hypocrisy, injustice and sterility . . . wasn't surprising at all that a spirit as liberated as his would pay the awful price of all the fetters that bind our own.

They put him to a brutal death—even we could not have done it better—but ever after they have as a result made suffering effective because of him.

When Jesus had gone back to the Father, to *that glory which I had with you before the world was made*, his heart was really still here with us so he sent us the Spirit of himself and his Father to work in our lives and help us understand the deep truths for which he had given his life. The Holy Spirit so empowered our suffering, because of the one who had died for love, that quite literally through this Spirit we learn, develop, progress, grow—step by step, infants that we are, falling, getting hurt, picking ourselves up, but yet achieving.

Our society may be disposable, but not our tears. They do not go to waste ... they purify us ... put us on holy ground ... water our starving roots ... wash our relationships clean.

And so, inevitably, I came nearer to the spirit of all the truths I had once taken for granted: I learned to kiss the cross, and mean it. I learned to say thy will be done, and mean it. I learned to establish the right priorities and to be proud of nothing because I have nothing, except what he has given me. Above all I learned to be grateful, and to show appreciation for life, for time, for health, for love, and for my cleansed and deepened relationship with God.

If there is a dividing line between love and pain, I have not found it yet. Suffering is nothing but love, a holy person once said to me, and love, after all, is what we are here to learn. Perhaps some learn it by work ... but the way of pain is much quicker and surer; it opens you to yourself, to others, to God, and it leaves no room for self-deception or self-glory.

Together love and pain are the time when faith becomes *Faith* . . . when only that is whole which has been broken down to dust. The props you once relied on shatter and scatter and you are forced to look within yourself for meaning and mastery. There quite simply you meet God, the Person who is the Name, in the defeating darkness of your own emptiness, in the desert through which you must go alone, in the pall of silence cutting you off from everyone and everything by the experience which you cannot share and must endure.

You do not even know at which point you opened the open door *wide* and he became your guest and you were sharing a meal together. You hardly look beyond the night anymore because of the wonder of the love reaching through; you know the dark lasts only a moment, then it is forever—and the pain is over.

But do not mistake my meaning. There is *no comfort* to be had from this time of deepened faith, though the mysterious "certainty" it imparts tells you there are no impossibles, or unexplainables, or unpurposables, or unanswerables; though the unfelt reality of his love is all around you and you have the light of a thousand eyes with which to "see." But comfort there is none.

If there were comfort in faith, would the victims of the Third Reich have cried out in despair *There is no God* ...? It would be easy then to believe and faith would mushroom everywhere and not be "gift" at all, degenerating into a spiritual drug to allay spiritual pangs, affording relief, escape, euphoria. Only believe and everything will come right! No ... when you believe best everything is worst. That is precisely why you believe. Not because of the glimmer of light but because of the impenetrable blackness.

When Jesus cried out in desolation on the cross *My God, my God, why have you forsaken me?* he knew his Father was still there, though he seemed not to be. That is the meaning of faith. I look at Mary and wonder whether knowing that God himself was at the bottom of all that was happening to her boy, God's Son, made the cruelty any easier to accept.... Faith is hidden in obscurity and its love on this earth is a love that is all pain, for it carves with a blunt knife and it touches the bone.

I went round the house crying to the silent walls and empty rooms: My Jack had CANCER . . . My Jack is DEAD . . . It isn't a dream . . . it's FOR REAL.

God. *God* . . . was all I could think and say and pray. Perhaps it meant *I love you*. Perhaps it meant *I'm sorry*. Perhaps one day I will be transported by this one word *God* that is now only a burden of agony.

In June one day, after the cobalt and three months before his death, I sat on Jack's lap and cried my heart out. I am so glad he saw me cry, at least that once. He held me gently, and when he thought I had cried enough he said: *Dar*ling . . .! as much as to say, there now, no more.

Remembering was something I couldn't face, though I kept remembering, so all day long I stopped short of him only letting in the smallest fraction of his unforgettable presence to my too-tender consciousness (I *loved* thee, but now I love thee not). I had shut him out in the cold—so I thought. Non time. Non space. Non Shirley.

But who is there from heaven on down who is proof against the power of love? Jack crept in with stealth and subtlety ... found ways of insinuating himself ... so that wherever I looked it was him I saw, and whatever I did and thought and remembered, him again. It was fully 18 months before I even began to realize that the only way to handle grief so that it serves you instead of masters you is by looking it in the face, letting it break you, not by looking for relief. Deciding to turn around and retrace the steps of my own Golgotha in their entirety was probably the most difficult thing I ever had to do in my life, but *that* was the time when I began to heal, and, more than that, be profoundly changed.

Today our priest has just come in while on his way to minister to another bereaved person. He hasn't the time to sit down so he just stops fleetingly in the passageway, takes both my hands, and says he is thinking of me. It is only a lightning visit but no doctor could have brought as much comfort or healing. My mind computes it under the heading J-O-Y.

Human joys are fleeting. They come and go like fireflies in the night, wrote a very dear and respected Jesuit priest who died recently in India. Unknown to me now the night will be all the blacker for this little spark now swallowed up beyond recapture.

But physical darkness soothes, unlike spiritual darkness, and times out of number I went out to the very private back section of our house to continue my solitary communion with the stars. If there was no moon to outface them, these unwilling worlds would materialize for me by the billion and even reach down to me as I opened my arms to the immensity in which they hung like flickering candle flames a single sob could extinguish.

Where was Jack among all those stars? Could he see me standing alone, my aloneness crying out to be known and found by him? Night after night I questioned the stars, yet all the while I knew the answer. But reassurance is a luxury, not a necessity. Often I wondered what grieving without hope would be like and whether I would be grieving at all if I could see things through other eyes and bring myself to believe there was no life, no conscious life, after death. If the love-bond between Jack and me was irrevocably severed, if he couldn't know how greatly he was loved and missed, my tears would indeed be running to waste and I would be better off to put them and him out of my life for good.

Other thoughts came back to me too, that I had played with for a long time. A private pet theory was teasing my imagination: that the moral order paralleled the material order and that planets of pure evil (hell) and planets of pure good (heaven) existed and that mixtures of good and evil like ours were the testing ground, matching the pure matter (stones, water), pure spirit (angels or intelligences), and in-betweens like us humans on this earth. Otherwise, *why* all those stars? I suppose I might as well ask, why so many thousands of species in a genus! No one can hold creation back and say *Enough*! as it testifies to God's immensity.

Thank you for the gift of faith. I may not feel its comfort, Lord, but I understand its purpose. Let me be to you as nothing who are everything to me. And if at the end of this solitary struggle the murkiness empties before all the riches of the depths of God who sees me only with the eyes of love and therefore as my best self, then wonder upon wonder will open to me as I behold the wealth of your love and in it my own.

So gradually my premature effort to know eternity deepened my belief in the continuity of life, and little by little my estranged sense of time returned to normal—I forced myself to go on winding the clock—though looking at all those stars could throw it out of focus again.

Time is very deceiving anyway. Look at us for example. While we were away for three months visiting family and friends in Holland and the United Kingdom the year after our marriage he was already growing the seeds of death and neither of us knew it. I may look back now and say yes, this or that was the writing on the wall, but without the prespective of time we would never have come to recognize the condition that needed that very time to develop. What an irony.

I filled an album with photographs, all of them happy ones, and Jack always the star of the piece, Koos this, Koos that, and their hi's illuminating the eye of the camera, all of them so real they could just about walk out of the celluloid.

One of those smiles at least must have been forced . . . must have known deep down that all was not well. . . . The lie of the firefly. It must have known those photographs would be all I would have.

But though my camera caught their vital, alive faces, full of fun, full of living, and all the nuances of expression words could never capture, it is still too difficult to look at them because I look with my heart. One day perhaps the pictures will live for me once more and, like the beautiful plant on my table that has developed over generations the cunning outfit it wears, and must wear always, they will never be sad in my memory, or angry, or afraid, or anything but happy, just as they are in these pictures.

Once, after we knew the worst, I caught Jack looking at them, the only time he had ever shown any interest, and he quickly put them away. I wish I had been able to tell him then how I felt, how I shared his deep feeling, how the memory of Father standing windblown on the wharf to welcome us was something I would never forget. But communicating true feeling was something I learned only after death had visited my home. . . .

In view of all that happened, how grateful I am we saw Jack's parents when we did, and I took the pictures I did. By the end of that year Mother would be dead, and just ten months after her Jack would be dead too, followed by Father six days later, "together now" as an old priest commented.

My beloved cheat, on your walks with Father in Alphen on the Rhine, when I trailed you with my camera and laughed when you laughed though I didn't understand a word of the conversation, were you then planning this rendezvous?

How bitterly I have blamed our trip for all the pressures it put on you, commuting, commuting, commuting. You had to see it all, every art gallery, every museum. Remember the National Art Gallery in London? I persevered resolutely from room to room with you for four hours, bone weary, my nerves ragged with the strain, so relieved it was all over at last—only to find we had just been on *one floor*. You went back the next day, alone.

———————

Soon it was July and we were flying home with Singapore Airlines on Jack's birthday. I whispered this singular bit of information to the chief stewardess and she disappeared at once, then returned with a plastic bag which she presented to him. He put his head down smiling broadly in pleased embarrassment, but he was a big boy and he was not going to open his present. So I had to do it for him. Inside: a magnetic chess set, a magnetic checker set, and four packs of Singapore Airlines playing cards. A real thrill!

Then ... 7 p.m. and touchdown. Ten loved and familiar faces, soon becoming babbling voices, were there to welcome us—you'd think it was summer all over again instead of midwinter. Hugs and kisses all round: Raewyn and her husband, Gay, Norman and the children.

But the idyll was really over and it was the beginning of the end. Jack started having night sweats ... the electric blanket, we thought. Then we moved at the end of November and there was all the work on the house we bought ... six weeks of it, an orgy of painting, papering and adaptation, Jack absolutely in his element, not to speak of the less-creative cleaning jobs which I vigorously and wholeheartedly attacked myself.

The reek of chemicals was overpowering and it brought on a fearful attack of asthma during which I fought for every breath in lungs that seemed banded by iron. But Jack had been breathing chemicals for 25 years or so, and I doubt if he ever bothered about good ventilation when he was working on the interior decoration of new homes as I found to my sorrow the day I went to the work site with the doctor's summons.

The confusion was so confounded that a visiting cat, slipping in one day for a peep at the new arrivals, took one look at the unbelievable mess, turned and went for her life, terrified, her tail hoisted like a mast, her hair standing on end! I got quite hysterical over it. Surely we weren't as bad as all *that*.

I have heard of the sudden flood of energy before dying but I could never have known all this was an example of it. During this time we ate makeshift meals mostly, Kentucky-fried and fish 'n' chips appearing frequently on the menu—God, how I blamed myself afterward.

Jack was always overheated at night, but it *was* well into summer (December-January). Then I noticed the flesh was falling off him. When I put my arms around him, he was only a bag of bones.

I had to get him to the doctor, but the trouble I had doing it. Like so many men he would have nothing to do with doctors. Waste of time in his opinion (they'll only finish you off). But his left toes were very sore with a rash that would not heal, and that really got him down. What was happening to the good blood he had always boasted about ...? So I capitalized on this.

When the appointment was made I wanted to go with him but he wouldn't have it. He was already too ashamed to be going to the doctor for such a "trivial matter"—his words, spoken with contempt. I therefore telephoned privately and requested a thorough checkup for him. I knew he would never ask for one himself. The foot condition turned out to be crucial ... indicative of something else. This, and the puffy, inflamed roots of his fingernails. The specialist took one look at Jack's hands—commending the G.P. who had "spotted" it and referred him—and he knew it was the chest. Then the X-ray left us in no doubt. O my God, the shock of it.

Raewyn told me later that all his life Jack had had a dread of cancer. But this was only the beginning. Yet when it became as bad as it could be, he was able to cope and endure, and more than that, to grow. Without a word he hid away his pipe and ashtray and I did not find them again till after his death. This symbolical action was ironical because Jack used to say jokingly he would never give up smoking even if he got cancer.

The pity of it however ... that fear, shock, anger, shame, guilt, can fortify our wills, and love cannot or will not, even the love of our own lives.

Then it began: first one hospital for tests, then another for surgery, and a third for cobalt, all very specialized, the treatment throughout superb. They did everything they could but it was really too late, and the cancer meanwhile was accelerating from primary to secondary.

Too late ... even for God? I didn't understand then as I do now those words of Jesus about the grain of wheat:

> I tell you most solemnly, unless a wheat grain falls into the ground and dies, it remains only a single grain; but if it dies, it yields a rich harvest (John 12:24).

How insignificant a single wheat grain is. Neither a farmer's nor an artist's dream. Not even a meal for a bird.

But plant it or crush it—then you have a different story. Its death in the dank earth, its swelling and splitting apart, gives it a new identity which could not have happened without the disintegration of the old. The miracle of being made new is in the seeming destruction, the loss of self, but not of selfhood, the death on earth from which birth in heaven arises.

Jesus, his death closing in, knew the value it would have for humanity. Those who have followed him, whether knowingly or unknowingly, have not refused love by hoarding themselves. They have burst open in spontaneous joy of giving, or broken open in pain of hard surrender, but they have not remained closed.

God, who is Beauty itself, fills up into loveliness and goodness the empty husk of each broken grain, now rising toward him by the million like a shimmering ocean in full flood. He has invited us to share in the great feast when the harvest is done.

But it would take me a long while to comprehend the magnitude of all this, to experience the reality of God at

117

work in my life through Jack with a growing awareness and certainty that almost made faith redundant.

No, for God it is never too late.

Still, as long as there was hope of life, life as we knew it was all I could think of. Surgery and radiotherapy are drastic treatments. When it was all over my greatest regret was that I had accepted them without question because I cannot fight off the feeling that he might then have lived another two years. On the other hand, if he had died soon all the same, I would have blamed myself for not making use of whatever treatment was available. Either way I could not have escaped the agony of mind I endured.

The house became the first scapegoat in my abyss of self-reproach during the first years after Jack's death, and side by side was the guilt I experienced for having allowed it to happen. Believing I had full control of my life I imagined that somehow I had lacked the foresight and judgment that could have averted the tragedy.

So easy to fool ourselves until we

discover our impotence. That little nail for want of which a shoe—a horse—a rider—a battle—a kingdom were lost is the daily record of the multiple seemingly insignificant circumstances beyond our rational control.

One by one the platitudes drifted in about "all those beautiful memories" for which I should be grateful—torture by refinement. Shirley, they are saying, think how proud Jack was to finish it for you. He was *happy* doing it. And you went to Europe too. You met Jack's family. You had two wonderful years together.

Doing it FOR WHAT? *I don't want it.*

And I don't want any memories of Europe, damn them. All I want is to unlive the past year and to *stop* remembering.

God, I prayed, please grant me oblivion. . . .

If only I could sleep, then I would not remember.

If only I could die, then I would sleep forever.

God did not hear this cowardly prayer, of course. Instead, he let the answers come with time when hindsight brings the benefits into focus, as is the case with all disaster and loss.

Where did the diamonds catch their sparkle in their woody graves and cradles of coal? Who made the caterpillar airborne on wings of spun pollen? The way God responded to my darkness was his way, and I know now he was creating beauty far beyond the short-lived glory of a dawn or sunset cascading across the heavens and then dissolving from view.

If I could choose, retrospectively, all the ins and outs of my life, I would leave well enough alone, only amending those in which I had fallen short. As far as God is concerned, whatever he has done he has done *well* and I would continue to leave everything up to him as to one who knows best and loves most.

In those early days of bereavement I was sustained by feelings of deep gratitude for the almost incredible way events took shape, the details interlocking more securely than the sutures of a welded skull. Everything was "under control" yet neither I nor anyone I knew had anything to do with it. The following example is one that particularly stands out.

A friend of Gay's was on her way to Jack's funeral having heard about this "wonderful fellowship" I was experiencing which made her feel she had to be there though she hardly knew me at the time. But her car broke down. Would her colleague Mary give her a ride? Yes, of course Mary would.

After the burial, over cups of tea, I learned that Mary was indirectly related to the Koers family. No miracle here, not yet. When Mary got home, however, it began in the shape of a long letter she wrote to her sister Pieta in Driebergen (Holland) describing the funeral of a stranger that had somehow moved her.

The day that letter arrived Mary's sister was out in the shopping center where quite by chance she ran into Jack's sister, who is also called Pieta and also lives in Driebergen. They exchanged pleasantries and news. How is your father? asked Mary's Pieta. He has just died, answered Jack's Pieta, and what's more, our brother Koos has just died too in New Zealand.

On her return home Mary's Pieta found a thick letter in the mailbox, a strange letter, pages and pages of it—who was this "Jack" Mary was writing about? A beautiful letter, but.... Suddenly the penny dropped and she realized it was *Koos*, Pieta's brother! This was *his* funeral in New Zealand Mary was writing about!

Jack's Pieta was dumbfounded when Mary's Pieta telephoned the contents. Please copy it out for me, she begged. And that is how Jack's family had a firsthand, uninvolved, impartial account of their brother's funeral. I cannot write a word of Dutch. Who but the Lord could have arranged a little miracle like that?

How many wonders you have done for us, O Lord, our God!

How many plans you have made for us!

You gave us the marvels of outer space long before telescopes could register the grandeur of the constellations, and even before puny man was there to be overwhelmed by them.

Before even microscopes could unveil the secrets of minispace—each snowflake a six-ray patterned jewel, different from every other snowflake—you were within, and within, and within. . . .

No time machine could unravel even a fraction of the Unknown, yet you could put all knowledge into a lightning-flash of eternity. . . .

No hazardous ascent of the Olympian heights could reveal ways of getting to you, no journey to the stars at the speed of light could prove you are there. . . .

But here in our earthy, ordinary, routine-bound lives you work wonders greater than all wonders, teaching us the wonder of you, of your love, forgiveness, tenderness, compassion. This is true knowledge . . . all the knowledge I want.

The Pharaohs had not yet been mummified in the pyramids when underground rivers were fashioning their limestone masterpieces with delicate roseate tear-drippings of living rock, yet you knew of the creation of my inmost self, my knitting together in the limbo of the womb. No regression under deep hypnosis could reveal to me the mysterious complexity of my own being, the word not even on my tongue before you already know what I will say—and why I say it.

Not in a million years could I so know myself or understand the needs that lie open to your view.

If I were helpless like the lost sheep, you would somehow find me and lift me to the safety of your shoulders. Or if I were the barren fig tree lying under threat of being cut down, this same good shepherd, now good husbandman, would plead for one more year of tending to add to the other three *in case* this time it bears, almost taking the blame for the lack of fruit.

If I flew to the point of sunrise, or westward across the sea, you would be there to lead me, you would be there to help me.

You had my Jack with you always and now he has inseparably found you too. You have shown him to himself the way you dreamed him before earth took its toll—*because* earth took its toll.

I am almost ecstatic, Lord, when I think of all the strings you pulled. Jack had his sister Maartje here and his brothers Paul and Hans away, just as the brothers would have wished; he died in his own bed with me beside him, holding him; he was buried by the priest who had received our wedding vows and his baptismal promises (just a few more days and Father would have been away from Napier on business and later away altogether on transfer); the priests we had met in Wellington and Palmerston North both "just happened" to be here at the time of the funeral.

And I am only one of uncounted numbers who have experienced this caring at a death in the family.... His loved ones are very precious to him and he does not lightly let them die.

To me the way time held for Jack seemed almost like a miracle. When will it be? I asked the radiotherapist before we left Palmerston North for the last time on Saturday, September 23. Very soon, he replied.

Four days later, on his own request, Jack renewed his commitment to Jesus in baptism; then he also received the sacraments of confirmation, reconciliation and anointing of the sick. But for the partaking of the Presence under the form of bread and wine we wanted a special occasion to share with all our friends. The nearest free available date for our priest was Wednesday, October 4—a whole long week to wait.

I looked at the very slight but unmistakable swelling round Jack's right temple and quailed. My God, would he be able to last the week? Lord, what are we to do? I prayed. Should we wait for a public service or let him receive holy communion privately and soon?

Within seconds Faith took over, and Trust. The 4th was the Feast of Saint Francis of Assisi, the wonderful lover of all God's creation from the most dispensable cricket singing to the shyest wild flower, to the remotest, grandest star. If this was the day the Lord himself had chosen, I had nothing to be anxious about.

———

Today our priest has come again and this time he sits down. Shirley, he says, promise me you won't make any major decisions for a year, or at least six months. Ah ... these are the "stability zones" I read about later: the children, the house, one's employment, the city one lives in, and so on, and so on. The widow is almost toppled when her spouse dies and nothing in her entire life could possibly have prepared her for the devastation, unless she had experienced it before.

If you have never known the irreversible loss of a close relationship you cherish, then it is beyond your power to comprehend the desolation. The need to forget, to plunge recklessly into thinking of other things, becomes very pressing indeed ... ESCAPE ... call it what you like.

Anything but *this*. You cannot yet cope with the magnitude of your loss—just a little at a time, so much, no more. It was good that I made that promise or I might have followed my blind impulse to get back into the air: India ... Australia ... the United States ... *any* destination AWAY from here ... *anything* to STOP THE PAIN.

It is now early November, a month

since Jack's death, and our priest has come yet again, this time with an invitation. Shirley, he says, I have been asked to give a talk at the college this evening on the meaning of suffering in our lives. If you feel like coming along—no pressure—you'll be very welcome.

I do *not* feel like going along. All day long I toy with the idea, giving myself all the reasons why I do not want to go. I hadn't followed that particular renewal course for one thing; I had already done a Life in the Spirit seminar for another; I didn't want to meet all those people. Then *why* did I put reasoning aside and consider emotively how ungracious it would be to stay away when I had been personally invited?

On the table before us was an unpruned rosebush and our priest stood before it with a pair of shears, eyeing it purposefully. Then he set to work on it, commenting all the while on God's pruning action in our lives.

The shrub looks healthy but it lacks form and beauty. Too many leaves (cut), too many random branches (cut,

cut). If this shoot is cut away, that one will have more light. Spacing prevents overcrowding (cut, cut, cut). All the dead bits have to go ... all the diseased parts. There's a method in all this madness, the *future* plant. It will have a strong framework ... be healthy and beautiful. God is at work in our lives. *He is in control*. We don't understand now but we are being brought to our full potential. Nothing is taken away without a purpose. It hurts, it hurts terribly, but it has a meaning....

My words are only shadows of his. I don't remember what he said, yet I remember the message indelibly. The meaning of the image of the rosebush being pruned is part of the substance of my whole self and life, my extended self, with all its affections and relationships impregnating my "subtle body." This is what will survive forever; this is what, in Christian terms, will rise to glory, and so must be purified and made beautiful.

With great humility he then gave us a glimpse of the interior suffering in his own life 18 months before his ordination. The light went out and never came back again, he said. He was under medical care for a time and he feared his superiors would not allow him to be ordained but they did, and his joy was so overwhelming that he wept throughout the ceremony.

The pain of loss had made me very vulnerable—and this was dynamite. These weren't just words. This was a person in whom Jesus was alive, *really alive*. I am so moved, I said to him after the talk, I am going to write a poem for you.

If I were one of those unusual people who have what is called extrasensory perception, I would not have gone to that talk. I would have known that my stripping, begun at Jack's death, would mercilessly continue till everything I touched was taken away or turned to bitterness. I would have known that my life would never be the same again. This was the challenge of faith and, even if I wanted, there could now be no turning back.

Till now I had been content to be an

unpruned rosebush, quite at home with the flaws and blight. Then God had come along and *cut* into my being's core ... had thrown me from my safe, secure spiritual rut ... had wielded and was still wielding that relentless knife, tearing away branch after branch as he left me bare, robbed of every anchor except him, and still crying, though less for the pain and more for the wonder of the greater love now struggling in.

Lord, once a spoken word changed water into wine. Now by the same Word, this time unspoken, change me, not for my sake but for yours, from a wind-blown rosebush and a broken root into one of your little miracles. A perfect rose on a perfect tree.

5

The Need
to Grieve

Must I like an oyster
repose in the shell
hearing only the dumb
scream of the sea-surge outside,
moving me against knowledge
and perhaps will
to new hesitations, new graves;
Or shall I let in, now,
a small grain of sand,
suffer its torment
and harden this sickness
to pearl?
   Lee Tzu Pheng—*A Thought*[1]

A S long as Jack was alive it was
impossible to know how I
would feel once he was actually

dead, even though, during the eight months he was terminal, I sometimes forced myself to think of it, to try to picture life without his earthly presence. But when it finally happened I was only an infant, a novice, in a dimension I could never have imagined. Beside this life-sized wound that inflicts pain but doesn't kill, the hurts of a lifetime are just so many scratches and bruises. It is easy to understand why cultures devoted to minimizing labor and maximizing ease find the intensity of grief beyond endurance and must either camouflage it or dismiss it entirely.

One way of never getting hurt is never to love, never to allow oneself to care, never to open the door. The dark side of grief can be so frightening that shutting out love seems the best security for being spared the shattering feeling of helplessness that turns you in on yourself and makes you reject the will to live. The majority do love, however, and so are marked to know grief. And a majority, I hope, discover its bright and holy side . . . its power to cleanse, heal, strengthen . . . to give victory over areas of deadness in us while love is totally reborn.

But in the beginning grief was only negative—I thought. Depression was ugly, so was self-pity, so were all the concomitant emotions of anger, guilt, remorse, resentment—I thought.

None of this was directed against God, yet I hated what I saw and didn't know my view was distorted. Even if it had been directed against God, he is intelligent enough to interpret the situation. This is not meant to be flippant. Too often our attitude to God shows we do not give him credit for even the limited understanding and sense that we claim for ourselves. There is no way out of grief. I knew I had to face it. Endure it. I was too honest to run away for long. With this came the synthesis, the resolution, the phoenix rising renewed from its own ashes, for newness presupposes brokenness as resurrection demands death. I discovered all this for myself with something like the impact of a revelation.

One idea that fascinated me was found in the little pocket-book entitled *My Way of Life*, Saint Thomas Aquinas'

"Summa Simplified for Everyone," given me a long time ago by a dear Jesuit friend.

Here grief is described as one of the "emergency emotions" along with anger, hope and fear, because it is associated with difficulty. In today's language an emergency emotion would certainly be a coping emotion, and the energy it releases helps you to deal with the stress involved in a strife situation so that you are able to make the required effort to overcome the difficulty successfully. I have never lost possessions so I do not know how I would feel if fire, flood or burglary took them away from me. But they are never irreplaceable, and while you love them, they cannot love you back, so to lose them is not to lose love. The loss of a cherished relationship, on the other hand, opens the door to something much more serious—heartbreak. A sojourn in a dark valley, a walking through fire.

Here you have left the realm of the purely material and entered that of the psychological and spiritual. You have lost not only a person, but a person's love, and that takes something away from you that leaves you very poor. Lonely in your soul. Empty. All this creates a very difficult situation, a psychological state of emergency. Extreme sadness takes a hold of you and in this misery it is scarcely possible to experience any pleasure, let alone feel any joy. You simply have to accept realistically that for a long while you will not be able to enjoy anything because this depression will not go away overnight.

But the source of self-help arises from this very emergency situation; it is within us *in the shape of our own grief.*

To think we cannot cope is to have failed to tap our unlimited potential for rising to the occasion, for responding to the situation in a way that finally helps us to get the better of it. For example, a shy person is a fearful person. It is not easy to confront what frightens him, much less to overcome it. But if he thinks his self-respect is worthy of the effort, he may get up sufficient will power to make himself take that risk (of making a fool of himself) or shoulder that responsibility (when he may not succeed). If no great difficulty were involved then you could hardly say he had shown great courage in trying.

So too the person who is laboring to reach a worthwhile goal. He keeps on trying, against all odds, because the hope of labor rewarded, the confidence that he will eventually succeed, won't let him stop. I know if I had realized the tremendous commitment that writing a book entailed—especially one of this nature—I might not have had the temerity to begin, so I don't think I can claim courage for this endeavor. Call it sheer foolhardiness! But also call it love, with a great mixture of perseverance. If you believe in something you will naturally strive for it, toward it, on account of it, for the sake of it, whatever.

All life has to do with striving. You strive to attain, and when you have attained the object of your desires you strive to keep, and if you lose your treasure you strive to recover your loss, and if you can't recover it, you strive to accept. Anyone who has lost anything of value knows the striving that goes into the search: notices in the lost column, rewards offered for strayed pets, prayers offered, hopes fostered. In bereavement a person has been lost who will never again be found.

Yet something or someone must be found to fill that awful void so that it does not sicken, and that quest can be the beginning of philosophy: *Know thyself*. And this is the most sweeping, searching, grueling striving of all.

Few mourners, I think, would escape the very negative time classified as depression, or the self-pity that usually accompanies it as a normal and integral part of grieving. But only the bereaved person knows how appallingly distressing it is as it bites into your self-respect, savaging your ego, and exposing the frail stuff of which you are really made. Could this unwholesome brew of seething, conflicting emotions really be *me*? The resentment, the spite, the alienation?

I needed more faith to believe in my intrinsic lovableness than in the dispersion of the angels like nuggets of gold light throughout the cosmos. Also more faith to believe in my future. Happily the froth was all coming to the surface, being recognized for what it was, and cleared away.

Shirley, you have been given strength, our priest observed while I was attending Jack in his last hours, but where is my strength *now*? If I look inward I am sick at the sight of all I see, if I look outward the inner fires are further stoked.

He was right, however. The Source that never runs out hidden within me was there for me to draw on whether I asked for help or didn't, whether I couldn't or wouldn't ask for it. Asking is nevertheless recommended by Jesus himself and though I didn't pray for myself at this time I am sure others did and I thank them now.

The more deeply I grieved once I was definitely into it, the more my weaknesses were laid bare like suppurating carbuncles; but at the same time I was the more effectively cleansed of self-interest, selfishness, arrogance, negativity, till those words of Jesus to Saint Paul—My grace is enough for you: my power is at its best in weakness—really came alive for me. I was making the remarkable discovery that there is nothing negative about grief except its outer aspect, that this seemingly tottering foundation is the *rock* on which the positive is built.

But if I am to write about it sincerely, as I would like to do, I must go back to the gathering in my home after the funeral as a sort of launching pad to describe the growing feelings of isolation and antipathy. The hospitality was organized by the Catholic Women's League and I here express to them my heartfelt thanks, and also to all those who so thoughtfully contributed to the general refreshment. It was heartwarming to see so many people, but my feelings of alienation and estrangement had unfortunately already begun.

There was a great sense of continuing unreality and the sight of them all, of people working in my kitchen independently of me, cut me off from them as if I had been a stranger. Everyone was talking to everyone else—I don't think they even noticed me, the outsider posing as a guest.

I went round smiling, even ministering to Jack's bereaved family. Did they think I didn't care? People everywhere, teacups everywhere. Will you have a biscuit? More tea? Yes, it is cold today, isn't it?

Everything was as strange and unreal as it had been when the family went to view Jack's embalmed body at the funeral parlor and I had kissed his icy forehead and held his marble hands, the ring I hadn't removed still shining on his finger, while the others held back from his open casket and Hans had shouted out: *He'd look better on his feet*!

I imagined I could feel their shock because I was smiling down at the form that was his but yet not him.

I was sure they thought I didn't care.

Nobody asked me about Jack at that funeral gathering, and I did not speak about him. I remember wishing I could have cried in front of everyone so they wouldn't be so casual, so they would know how I really felt—and comfort me.

Funny how common experience levels all differences and when there is no such unifying bond everything else one has in common, language, culture, religion, can be very superficial.

Remembering how I felt on this most desolate day of my life, I am now very careful to seek out the bereaved person whose home I may be at for the coming together and ask: How do you feel? I learned the question from our priest and it never fails to open the door to true communication. The request: tell me about him or her, also brings an immediate response.

One cannot blame people for holding back from a grief-stricken person when they feel out of their depth; after all, how would a nonmedical person like myself feel in the presence of the victim of an accident or of a dreadful disease?

Even when fortified by experience it is still very difficult to approach an acquaintance on that more intimate basis of the touch of a hand or eye contact, especially when the occasion is as dismaying as that of a bereavement. The embarrassment is so great a barrier to overcome that most people either fall back on trivia or instinctively observe the golden rule of silence. These are actually easier for the griever to accept, as is also the helpless expression of inadequacy "I don't know what to say," than are the platitudes.

At least you had those two wonderful years.... It would be harder to take if you had been married longer (imagine that). You are lucky he did not suffer too long (as if eight months and one week were not long enough).

Yes, but what has all this got to do with his death? You are giving me all the reasons why I should *not* grieve, not why I should, and believe me *I must grieve* if I am to get over it.

Speaking for myself, the person who conveyed sympathy to me very gently and sincerely was a former colleague of mine who just held me close without a word, and then I saw the tears in her eyes. This is the sort of sympathy that becomes a memory because it so beautifully *consoles*, and it taught me that the instant rapport of touch cannot be improved upon.

I have asked myself many times which would help more toward acceptance and growth, the casual attitude of the community that expects you to cover up and get on with living as if nothing has happened, or the more caring attitude that gives you listening support and recognizes that for a long time you will not be your normal self. The truth of the matter is that though you have indeed to get on with living, and go on responding to others living around you, you cannot in honesty behave as if nothing of consequence has happened, as if everything is "just fine."

It *has happened*, as one woman was forced to admit, though only in her sleep. *Then* her family knew from her dream sobs how deeply she was feeling the loss she could not and would not show in her waking hours for fear of the embarrassment of being seen yielding to emotion. This kind of conditioning is not helped by the subtle pressures well-meaning people put on you to pretend you are all right when you aren't, because of the brightness of their own approach, and it greatly increases the stress of grieving because it underlines how totally alone you are, even when surrounded by those of your own flesh and blood.

I was surrounded only by family in the Lord and I too experienced many unreal attitudes. I also experienced much kindness but unfortunately during my negative period the less-pleasant memories took over and I disregarded the kind supportiveness of the charismatic prayer group I had attended for a time and allowed myself to become harshly critical of the way "they"—the whole, nebulous, worldwide movement—gloss over the severity of grief by what I call the artificial glorification and ritualizing of joy.

Clap, you have so much to be grateful for, one woman whispered to me a month after the event, while another enthusiastically seized my arm and shoved it up in the air at a large meeting I was fool enough to attend, leaving my feelings so violated that I quite unfairly held the whole movement responsible for the insensitivity and tactlessness of some of its members whose zeal overruled their compassion.

Not surprising then, that a barrier develops between you and the world at large and between you and your brothers and sisters in the Lord. It is all very well for me to glory in being a child of God and to make "He touched me" the occasion of my joy, so long as I don't manifest arrogance in my sense of privilege and discount by implication his work among the unchosen who are subject to sickness and grief and all the frailties of human nature because they haven't been healed!

The Holy Spirit will get you yet! exclaimed one charismatic gentleman patronizingly—as if he wasn't with me already through baptism and confirmation and a life of commitment, and as if my salvation and sanctification depended solely on my being a member of their group.

I have great respect for the charismatic renewal, the freshness it has brought to Christendom; I even freely acknowledge its initial influence on my prayer life. But I resent the way a bereaved person was "held up" at a gathering for the courage and cheerfulness with which a death in the family had been "accepted" when the truth of the matter was that that person was still in shock and the loss had not even begun to register.

It must be clearly understood that the expression of grief in no way diminishes or negates the fact of acceptance and courage, and no one need be ashamed of the tears any more than that person would be embarrassed if others saw the smile of delight in a beautiful day or heard a chuckle of amusement at a good joke. The Lord of us all is happy to have us whether crying, laughing, working or recreating. The church has recognized this all along and channeled our feelings in liturgical worship: the Christmas crib, the Good Friday passion, the exultation of Easter.

Nothing can be more limiting or claustrophobic than group ties coming on top of denominational ones and reinforcing human differences instead of the unifying good news of Jesus. We do not have to be for Peter, Paul or Apollos in order to be full, mature Christians. Church groups are good, all a means to an end, as long as they never become an end in themselves or take allegiance away from where it really belongs, with Jesus our King and Lord, the bridegroom of the whole People of God. And it is not our place to pin the label "saved" on anyone because we cannot manipulate God or restrict his grace.

Death is incontrovertible, a fact of history and biology; but grief is something else. We can actually turn our back on it by choosing, as some do, to drown our misery in alcohol, dose ourselves with drugs, fall headlong in love on the rebound, lose ourselves in a desert of sterile activity, put on a brave front, and flaunt that stiff upper lip. We can cover up, immerse ourselves in work (as I did), go on a holiday, get back into the stream of things as if we had never left it, pick up the threads where we left off, as if it had never happened. Worst of all, we can even pretend the heresy that our grief is "really nothing," in the hope it will go away if we behave as if it isn't there. A clutched straw to anesthetize the unbearable pain.

It won't go away, of course ... not until the wound is probed and cleansed, and the grief gently redirected. It will burrow into us, and nature's perfectly designed safety valve could refuse to function.

Very real symptoms might then begin to warn us that we are not recovering as we should, and we might learn to our cost that running away from the necessity to grieve is as unhealthy as morbidly clinging to grief and refusing to progress toward acceptance and peace. We might then find that learning to grieve constructively by allowing ourselves to hurt to the full is not an unwholesome luxury, definitely taboo as some imagine, but plain common sense; that by sincerely expressing genuine feelings, and feeling, we are not wallowing but keeping emotionally balanced—sane.

I remember a certain woman who came to one of the several little talks I was invited to give to various groups. She had experienced the loss of a parent two years previously. From her comment that she "felt guilty" if a single day passed without her thinking of her mother, because she wanted to "keep her memory alive," I knew something was wrong. I went to see her, and she talked and talked and talked. Then I asked her if she would like to talk about it to the Lord, and she started to cry— her first tears. When I saw her again a few months later she was radiant. Her tears once freed had gone on for days and the suppressed grief, now properly directed, was out of her system at last. She loved her mother and she had now paid the price we must all pay for loving. She had mourned her loss.

An extreme example of refusal to grieve came to my notice through the media and made me very angry at the time. The attitude seemed like deplorable snobbery, justifiably resented by non-Christians: I'm a Christian so I can cope. I will see him again in Jesus so I can take it.

I realize now my own grief had probably made me too harshly judgmental since you have to find your own way of dealing with grief and the person was undoubtedly in acute shock. But to think you can minimize the pain of loss for yourself by being as uninvolved as possible in your own grief *because* you are a Christian is to practice massive escape in my view.

Jesus could so easily have done that at the tomb of Lazarus where he was about to reveal himself beyond question as the source of life and master of death, yet he showed the feeling that befitted the occasion out of love for his friends, Martha and Mary . . . he mingled his tears with theirs. Jesus once pronounced a special blessing for those who mourn, promising that they *shall be* comforted. Shall be . . . because healing does not happen overnight in the ordinary scheme of things.

Grief is endemic in human affairs—the suffering is always there. Personal sorrow of one kind or another never goes away. There are not only the everyday tragedies on our own domestic scene but also the world-scale violence and exploitation in our tortured century, unable to rid itself of the demons that bring such horrifying destruction: cruelty, greed, hatred, lust. To grieve for the heartbreaking waste of human lives that find only darkness and sterility and total death must surely be an act of virtue that will ultimately release energy to build a better world. Perhaps by refusing to admit the presence of grief a bereaved person has indeed been "healed"—but have you *grown* from this magnificent opportunity to be broken in spirit with Jesus and learn in this testing ground of faith what Faith really means?

To be ashamed of grief is to misunderstand it, to think it is negative in itself and so must be put behind us as soon as possible in order to pick up and put together the fragments of a normal life in which only the good things are remembered. It is to treat it in some sense like a sickness or abnormality, which of course it is not—unless it is allowed to become morbid—so that it fails to be taken seriously by the person experiencing it. What a loss. *Come down from the cross*: that taunt is nothing new. It is because grief has such power to bog down that by the same token it can so greatly regenerate.

While it can destructively silence every other voice but its own, it can, under the Holy Spirit, help us to develop along completely different lines, or along the same lines but in a much deeper way. It unleashes feelings you never knew you had, and in an intensity you never would have thought possible. If your grieving remains futile and immature so that the negative aspects perpetually choke out the positive, so that you never come to peace, never find at least some of the answers deep down in your own heart, never learn to look outward to the suffering of your fellow creatures, then, not only do you not cope (though outwardly you may), and not only do you not grow, but your whole family and the community miss out too from all that you, and others through you, could have become.

To turn round and face the enormity of our sorrow takes courage, but how will we cope—how can anyone cope? Well, of course we can't, by ourselves, that is. Something, someone, some circumstance, must help to hold us together like the branch without which all the leaves would be blown away. Family, employment, paramedical services (if called upon), all play their part, but they are not enough.

Ultimately we are thrown on our own inner resources and *this* is where strength must come from ... from within our own grief ... the fruit of common sense, the will to live, the need of others and by others, the belief that a purpose is at work which we will one day understand. And this is where we learn the most difficult and strengthening lesson of all: that life does not wait upon our grief. It simply goes on regardless. We cannot just grieve. We have to *live* and grieve.

I knew instinctively there was an immense amount of learning to harvest from my loss and a whole new beginning was ahead of me if only I waited to discern it step by step and then took hold of it with courage when the perspective of time had revealed it to me. In retrospect I know my temporary withdrawal into a year's solitude was very worthwhile, even creative (because I was at this time researching a course I was to give[2]), enabling me as it did to confront the complex train of invading emotions and preparing me for the day I would be ready to put my experience to use for others.

My silence was broken only when I broke it, but eventually I did make a conscious effort to step back into the sunshine—a grace. And by then I was developing the gift of compassion, the best antidote to grief, and becoming increasingly involved with other people —another grace. In fact, in the years following the course I found I was using gifts I scarcely realized I had been given, especially in the area of speaking to various adult groups, and since I was simply responding to invitations, never seeking out opportunities or needs, and everything was pointing in the same direction, I would be naive not to recognize that God had given me a "work."

If you had asked me then, as someone did 20 months after the event, what stage of the grieving process I was at, I would have understood you because I had read all the "death books," but I would not have been able to answer. Nature needs four seasons to describe herself, and can the enormity of deep personal loss and of adjustment to it be conveyed in one trite sentence? I doubt whether I even went through the stages,[3] some of them yes, but not in order.

To begin with my grieving seemed riveted to guilt; holding myself responsible that my loved one was no more. God was above blame by wisdom, love and holiness, so it had to be me—I never thought of blaming Jack. And toward others too my feelings became increasingly negative as I experienced one disappointment after another. Stage two: Anger? Very potent and very unpleasant.

Guilt is devastatingly unpleasant too, a torture inflicted by love. I had known all about it since I was about nine. My little dog Rough died and I blamed myself for not helping him in time.

Some terminal patients may also feel guilt if they have practiced slow suicide through harmful addictions (to drugs, cigarettes, alcohol, high-cholesterol foods), but no amount of sorrow, or change of habit, can reverse what they have done to themselves. Jack, for example, was cured of smoking by the shock of being faced with the possible loss of his own life, but it was too late.

Remorse is tied up with guilt ... regret for what might have been, *if only*. I think part of the agony is the cry for a second chance. But of course, *in that situation* there will be no second chance. If only we hadn't gone overseas, my heart cries. If only I hadn't let Jack work so hard on the house. But today cannot undo yesterday. The worst part of the pain is always the realization that the person now gone was never fully appreciated.

My guilt feelings were not backed by any anger directed against God or myself, but they found a target in a lot of suppressed anger over my great disillusionment during the first year and a half about what I thought was the discrepancy between the theory and practice of love in Catholic circles. It is supposed to be of the authentic human variety: real warmth, real tears, real enjoyment of another's friendship, real reaching out; as far removed from detached do-goodism as is genuine openness to another, even at the risk of tenderness or passion; commitment to the point of involvement, discomfort, embarrassment, time, hurt.

We must be "in love" with people, we are told in renewal seminars, and not be afraid to let them be "in love" with us. The more I heard words like these the more cynical and angry I became because, as a widow, it seemed to me that fear, not love, was at the heart of our human relationships, making it quite clear that all this beautiful idealism was safe only as long as it was in the head. If any heart were in it at all, that would be a different proposition and psychological indicators might be needed to test the purity of our motives.

The abnegation of a limber saint like Jesus who loved in a deep personal way, and let himself be so loved, is better understood by the Eastern mystics who proceed from the love of their guru, the known, to the love of God, the unknown.

I realized with a jolt that I was only on the periphery—or so it seemed to me— with little real closeness between me and anybody and it made me wonder whether kindness was real loving or a cloak for condescension.

Bereavement also brought to light many self-contradictions that were not easy to deal with. For instance, I both wanted and needed to be left alone, but if I were left alone for a long period my self-esteem resented it and self-pity began to work insidiously. *So this was it. Nobody really cares after all.*

Friends were no doubt placed in an awkward position because of their uncertainty as to my needs. Since I preferred to continue on the basis of: If I want company I'll seek it, there was a tacit understanding with some of them that I would telephone if I needed to spend an evening with them. Once or twice I followed it up, but then I began to think I was getting too demanding. If they really cared, *they* would telephone, I would think bitterly, passing the buck.

What I only came to realize later was that it is as difficult on a different level for friends to cope with the bereaved person as it is for the bereaved person to cope with the loss; they want to help but simply don't know how, their very sympathy increasing their awkwardness. But friends only have to tune in ... and they need not underestimate even a vague and general offer of help because it indicates their willingness to be near and to be of service, and it greatly comforts the bereaved person and encourages her to state her needs, most of which will probably be of a practical nature.

Unfortunately, the extreme denial most people practice toward bereavement—it's just not there—makes them over-careful to behave normally and treat you normally so that they are quick to change the conversation if one of the little ones asks *Where's Jack?* not realizing that the avoidance of the beloved name thereby underlines it and robs you of the opportunity for sharing and release.

Speaking in general terms, the more friends try to spare you pain by the "kindness" of saving you and themselves embarrassment, the more uncomfortable they will make you feel till you could be reduced to considering yourself an intruder for having sought their company and returning home much sadder than when you set out.

It was no good becoming hurt and withdrawn. Equally futile too to blame myself for my disappointment, or try to rationalize the situation, or dwell on the pitifulness of human hopes that fade out like the illusory rainbow. If others couldn't make the adjustment, *I* would have to make it, it was as simple as that. But how negative it made me for a time.

The human in me kept asking what Jack and I would have done if anyone we knew had died instead of him, and the feelings that surged up to answer showed me plainly how much I had taken for granted and how automatic my expectations were. To have had none would have secured me against feeling hurt and let down. To have accepted the situation *as is* would have been to remain detached and free. Very difficult when you are in such a vulnerable and hypersensitive state and the people who reach out to you are perhaps not the ones you looked to.

So I had to learn that relationships are not static, always holding the same level of communication, and that nothing is more inevitable than that as a result of the death of a spouse personal relationships in general will be affected and changed.

To state it positively, personal relationships must move into a new understanding because your status has changed and so has your concept of life while that of your unbereaved acquaintances, who can no longer empathize with you and who may even find it hard to sympathize because of their conditioning, is still running along the same lines.

You must therefore accept that some friends will continue to invite you as they did when your spouse was alive, and others will not, though some, not so close before, will now draw closer and surprise you with the sincerity of their affection. You must even accept that your negative feelings about the general social pattern of friends of two seldom being friends of one could, perhaps, be true, but are more likely the result of your own inhibitions. In any case, it takes two hands to clap and if you hadn't withdrawn in the first place the ice would never have formed.

In fact, every bereaved person must accept that a lot of secondary hurts are tied up with the main one, which will rankle for a long time. This social, psychological death is the other face of the physical death disrupting your life and in time you will learn to rise above it— even be grateful for the whole experience. I am sure the griever too almost certainly inflicts hurt upon her friends, but they are in a far better position to make allowances since they are lucid and rational while she is not, and they should never make the mistake of taking personally any failure to pay them the compliment of calling upon them (the initiative should be theirs), or any anger that may be expressed either in general or in personal terms as indeed this anger must crystalize in some form if it is to cleanse effectively and become a means to peace.

The pity of it is that because of the prevailing ignorance about the workings of grief, and the lack of understanding between people and the reluctance to get involved, seemingly good relationships break down under the strain and never progress to depth and maturity. The fear of disappointment and hurt can be so real that one may instinctively refrain from seeking relief from the burden of grief.

One of the aspects of my negative period was my attitude to my church family. As I sat surrounded by people Sunday after Sunday the question would formulate itself without any conscious prompting on my part: Are these really my brothers and sisters in Christ? But thinking of people collectively is an unjust and misleading way to think of them because groups are made up of individuals and individuals pour out the gift of themselves everywhere and I received numerous touching examples of kindness from frends and even from people I hardly knew as well as people of other church fellowships: Mass cards promising prayers, a pot of ferns, little offerings of flowers from friends' gardens, a book on the 23rd Psalm and several little books of devotional poems, firewood, services, two theater tickets, an anonymous ten-dollar bill, and, carrying over to the big days, a homemade Christmas cake and an Easter egg.

One of my rarest moments came when a priest from the local seminary took me on a picnic to a scenic lake during the Christmas holidays. Are you sure it's all right and they won't toss you out of the Marist Order? I smiled into the telephone. Yes, it's all taken care of, he laughed.

At times like these the heart is so softened that it is easy to think big, easy to forget one is a natural solitary. Once I had learned to enlarge my personal attitude the love was there because I put it there, and I could then also receive it from others. Further, I was then able to see that my church family had grown in love in its own way just as I had in mine.

Yet I would like to say very strongly, even *angrily*, that everyone should recognize the place and value of these feelings of antipathy and not increase the mourner's sense of guilt by putting them down. I experienced a little of this corrective attitude and it only made me more antagonistic whereas a gentle leading toward gratitude would have been far more beneficial.

This is a very loving community, more so than most (I was told very early in my bereavement when I was thinking of moving away), and you are not yet ready to leave it. Not ready to leave it! I don't need this community any more than it needs me, I said arrogantly, becoming more alienated than ever because the speaker didn't have my vantage point.

It is all very well for every bereaved person to take full blame for the crisis of self-pity but it is not clearly understood that it is often other people's reactions, or nonreactions, to a bereavement that are responsible for bringing it on. People's attitudes don't change easily. It is the bereaved who are forced to change as a result of them, and to do this without bitterness is very very difficult.

One must clearly distinguish between loving idealistically and loving realistically, between a nice warm feeling of love "for everybody" that is not necessarily real, and love that is truly practical by being put into practice for the person in need. I remember my negative feelings when someone told me after nearly two years of widowhood: My husband and I often think of you and pray for you and we both feel very close to you. I couldn't help thinking: Do you know what a telephone call would have meant to me?

Some will pray for the "cloud" to be lifted from you, others will remark that you must now be "so lonely," or insist they know how you feel when they haven't a clue. When Jesus spoke about the need to forgive *from the heart*, he knew what he was talking about. All of a sudden there was so much I had to forgive (myself, others) and I couldn't do it—I, who thought I knew what loving was all about.

But the trauma of loss is not wholly interior and mental. Added to it are the emotional vacuum and the practical aspect which anyone who has been through it will tell you about. All this together makes grieving the most difficult activity one may ever be engaged in, presupposing of course that the departed one was loved. He isn't there any more and you have no one to dress up for or go out with. As you sadly send all his clothes away to charitable organizations you can't help perhaps doing the same with a lot of yours. Then, inconsistently, you may go off and buy yourself an evening dress which you can ill afford and are not likely to wear, at least for a long time.

My practical difficulties were such that there could not have been a better learning ground for exercising and growing in trust and gratitude. Seemingly insuperable problems left me feeling as helpless and defenseless as an axolotl trying to redesign the Napier Aquarium, such as the time there was the recurring phenomenon of birds in Jack's studio and one dead thrush had upset me greatly. I hesitatingly mentioned it to a young woman from our parish who had cheered me with little visits and flowers, and she immediately enlisted her husband who enlisted the Young Christian Workers who fixed it for me without any delay— it was "only" the unfinished guttering, that's all, not even worth a raised eyebrow! They even poured some concrete for me after I had bought the cement, and I was so happy there were some bottles of beer left over in Jack's crate in the garage to make merry with, considering they would not even accept a donation to their favorite charity.

Apart from the leaden weight of sorrow in my heart, nothing about my precarious, chaotic, weed-dominated world really got me down except the sight of the weeds themselves ... WEEDS ... waging their untiring psychological battle—what was the use of *two* mowers when they were both temperamental and undependable?

This was a time when, in addition to physical weakness brought on by trying to go vegetarian (which I will tell you about in a later chapter), I was entirely without income. The sight of the advancing jungle almost killed me. But I did not let the weeds drive me out of our home. Though we had got the garden for Jack, I clung doggedly to the unwavering conviction that everything had happened, just as it had happened, for a purpose, and that one day it would be revealed to me. I don't think I ever asked the question WHY?

After all, hadn't I always maintained I had no problems?

No difficulty is insurmountable and a problem, to me, is something insoluble. If I can solve it, and I invariably can, then it's not a problem. I didn't solve mine alone—I would be the first to admit that. Community Work Schemes helped, so did kind people from the parish and Norman who removed truckloads of garden rubbish. I traded in the upsetting mowers as well as my rotary hoe for a brand new mower costing $335, but all I had to pay was $75. I was a new woman!

Still, from a purely practical viewpoint I was in a pretty hopeless position, at least at the beginning. My entitlements under the law were, I discovered, nil. To qualify for a widow's pension I would have had to be either ten years married or have a child of the union. I mention this only because it is invariably assumed, inferred, taken for granted that I must be on social welfare of one kind or another when I am very definitely NOT.

Till Jack's death I had never appreciated insurance, though I do grudgingly insure, but now I am wholly converted. Because of his foresight and perseverance in maintaining his life policy I now have an investment which gives me a small but steady income. But because it is bank interest it is taxable and I paid taxes with tears of blood even when my annual income was less than $1000 and my sole income! What is more, I paid them every six months because I was on a provisional scale. I managed only by selling off bits and pieces of equipment and by doing without everything I could possibly do without, including heating in winter, holidays and the like. I did not need to buy clothes and I sold Jack's car. Also, the house was mortgage-free and I had no dependents. Many would have said I was quite well off. Happily things did not remain like this for long, and I always seem to have more than I want or need. What came out of it for me was the realization of how it is usually possible to manage, given the will.

I was glad not to be in dire need of exercising my secondary teaching profession because I was not yet ready to go back to it. I had to have the time to be and become my true self, and I knew I had to write this book. Moreover, with the present surplus of teachers, I might not have been able to obtain a position and I would then have been tempted to take an unemployment benefit. This way

I actually save the government money by doing without a job I neither want nor need so they do not have to support the person who would have been done out of a job by me, a young person perhaps at the start of his career who, unlike me, had to make a home and accumulate experience.

It makes sense, though the system failed to appreciate my altruism and penalized me at every turn. Because I was not on social security I was always faced with full charges, though, mercifully, my rates were concessioned till I moved into a flat. Individual doctors were good to me else I could not have afforded even the occasional visit. And I have been very fortunate not to need either a dentist or an optometrist. Assets alone will not feed you or keep you in good health. Money is a vital component of grieving. To be without essentials is demeaning and it also puts a depressed person at great risk of seeking the ultimate solution, which in the end creates far more problems than it solves.

If I had been forced, prematurely, to

go back to working for pay I would not have been able to put five months of very developmental research into my course, or to have been enriched by interrelating with the community. I would never have fulfilled this deep need to commit my experience to paper, and above all, I would never have learned the preciousness of time, not for rushing and doing, but for being and becoming.

Time is a vital ingredient for being healed as well as for becoming a healer. If you want to help another you cannot do it unless you make yourself available, you cannot do it by refusing her a shoulder to cry on, as someone told me her own sister had done to her. You will only do it by turning your blind spot to the clock and so indicating your willingness to listen.

I remember standing on a drafty pavement outside a shop for well over an hour while a person I knew only by sight and name poured out the accumulated misery and frustration of two years of widowhood. I also remember two occasions when I myself appealed for a willing ear and Gay and another dear friend each came and spent with me all the time I needed.

Listening is sometimes all that is needed to bring comfort, and psychologists acknowledge the therapeutic value of confession or "telling." The one listening doesn't need to be apprehensive about what to say because there is no need to utter a single meaningful word or to provide any of the answers. Grieving people find the answers in their own hearts if they are given the chance to discover them by speaking them out, and especially if they are helped in this by sensitive and sympathetic listening on your part.

Incredibly too, you may be able to put things in a different perspective and so greatly ease the burden of grief. I had an experience of this which might be worth sharing here. A man had lost his wife after a long and very happy marriage. It was his second, his first wife having died tragically in her 20s. He was hurting terribly but he stoutly maintained he would "never be able to love again" ... he would "always be comparing her with N." ... so another marriage or relationship or friendship would be "selfish—just to keep away loneliness."

I felt very privileged that he was sharing this with me and there was very little I could say. And then the saving words tumbled out.... Why should you think like that? After all, if you had said that after your first wife died you would have missed the best part of your life—those marvelously happy years with your devoted second wife. If ever I saw a brow clear and a burden lift, I saw it then. His gratitude was touching.

Very sad to say, however, one of the most difficult gifts to receive is this kind of time and sympathy because it admits *need*. It is so easy to program oneself to believe one is not lonely when "hell, yes" would be far more honest. So there are those who carry on with the deeply ingrained grin-and-bear-it, rejecting their friends and church family and then perhaps revealing their depression to a total stranger.

One person recoiled from the proffered embrace and immediately herself took refuge in platitudes: No, no. We have all these beautiful memories. Another said: It's all right. We are a large family (as if having a large family could rationalize the loss of one member and make it easier to bear).

All this points clearly to the one important fact: It is not fully recognized that there *is* a need to grieve, a need to dwell lovingly and sorrowfully on one's loss, a need to receive comfort, and from that comfort, *strength*.

Christmas is the most vulnerable time of the year for those who have lost a loved one, and for me it was sweetened and softened by the kindness of those who invited me into their homes, undeterred by the size of their own families. Their fellowship brought home to me the essential oneness of all Christians through whom the brotherly love of Jesus is constantly reflected. By opening their hearts they shared far more than their table and greatly helped in the work of my rehabilitation.

The sympathy card, the condolence visit, the telephone call, are all good, but hospitality is better because sharing one's dearest earthly possessions, time and family, says more effectively than words: I feel for you, and I care enough to do something about it. Hospitality is better even when it is viewed with suspicion, as was my experience when my guest (a comparative stranger to this country who has since left) could not quite understand why I had invited her to dinner to express my sympathy. Trying to be attuned to others is not easy. You need abnegation to help you firmly shut the door on the hurt and disappointment you experience if they are not attuned to you, and your own recent loss is passed over as if it had never taken place.

It is understandable that if you are invited out at a time like Christmas you cannot enter into the festivities without pretense, and the joyful celebrations around you only emphasize your own unhappiness. But if you are not invited out you are going to be unhappy anyway. Even going to the post office or the supermarket will make you unhappy because they do not know your secret grief.

I remember a Christmas party I went to when I had been widowed a year and I felt my position was ambiguous because I was wearing my rings and the strangers I met would not have known unless I told them. People do not usually associate widowhood with a young person, or a younger-looking middle-ager, as if death were a respecter of persons. There is a lot to be said, therefore, for the old custom of wearing mourning which clearly establishes your social status, especially now when so many marriages end in separation and divorce, otherwise someone will make a remark that will leave him licking his wounds for the rest of the evening because he has been clumsy, and he didn't know.

How well I remember that first Christmas without Jack two months after the event. A special luncheon in the country—how often we had driven out that way—and, toward the end I had to leave the table. It's the wine, it's the wine, I sobbed as I ran from the room. I will never forget the sweetness of the hostess. She took me far out into the garden under the trees and walked with me silently while I slowly took a hold of myself.

Then dinner at Raewyn's. The tree, and beautiful presents showered into my lap. More snapped self-control.... Midnight Mass. And because I was already churned up I wept again. A gentleman whose wife had died on Christmas Eve two years earlier took the trouble to find out my name and address from the parish house and sent me flowers. Beautiful, beautiful flowers. Then he invited me out to a restaurant dinner. It made me feel like a special brand of human being again, a woman, and in comforting me I hope he found solace from his own pain.

At such a time it is all these unexpected kindnesses that really tie you up in knots, often very little things: a hand-loomed bookmark from the Third World Shop; a marzipan mouse; a pot of honey from a priest at the seminary; a letter that brings you the friend who wrote it; a charming pot plant; a surprise package of a visitor who arrives on a bicycle early on a cold morning, nose all red and hands all frozen, to help you weed your garden; sharing a turkey dinner with a family when you haven't the heart or will to force down a sandwich, let alone cook yourself a meal. No season is as heart-opening as Christmas, but I won't feel too guilty if I fail to welcome the new-born King with the joy others show, for in the season for everything this is my *time for tears*.

As I shape this chapter, four years have passed since Jack's tent that he lived in on earth was folded up, and he was taken to an everlasting home not made by human hands, in the heavens.

My true healing began when my true grieving began—about a year and eight months after his death when I started off and on to write this book. And slowly it became my landscape of relinquishment making me feel that right here within the four walls of my house I had evolved by a thousand years. Well might I then dream of shoes, suitcases and packing, always my dream symbols for change. At least in my own mind I had travelled a long distance. Very, very long.

My mind travels down the reaches of history. A mother saw her Son slowly die and suffered in her mind the pain of love in its direst extremity. Humanity's past, and all its mistakes. Its seemingly insoluble ignorance and intolerance. Its refusal to learn. Yet in spite of it all, the striving toward a better future, the very real growth and development of our human race as a whole.

And will there be a future . . .? No one can interpret the Mystery to anyone. One can only discover the truth of it for oneself alone. The meaning and the miracle. It would take more than the wisdom of Solomon to crystallize for posterity in a thousand idioms and images even one facet of the diamond's multidimensional translucency that is the mystery of God.

> All that he does is apt for its time; but though he has permitted man to consider time in its wholeness, man cannot comprehend the work of God from beginning to end (Ecclesiastes 3:11).

NOTES

1 This gem of a poem was sent to me by a friend. I have since tried to trace the source but without success.

2 I was invited to give a ten-week course on "Understanding Death and Dying" at Hawkes Bay Community College in Napier, New Zealand. I approached this from a secular standpoint, except for a philosophical look at death in the great religions of the world. This book gives me a chance to reveal the other side of the coin.

3 The familiar stages are listed by Dr. Elisabeth Kubler-Ross in her book *On Death and Dying*: denial, anger, bargaining, depression and acceptance.

6

The Point of No Return

At some moment I did answer *Yes* to Someone—or Something—and from that hour I was certain that existence is meaningful and that, therefore, my life, in self-surrender, had a goal.

Dag Hammarskjold—*Markings*

IN spite of a full, happy and very interesting life blessed with many warm personal relationships and the ability to put my heart into everything I undertook, my inner world remained essentially unchanged and true life satisfaction was not a reality, though at the outer level there was continual development. As yet I had only seen the sun colors in a cicada's wings and had no idea of the fineness of the human spirit, its capacity for carrying a rainbow in the heart, for self-regeneration, for never giving up.

The long phases of a terminal illness, the loss of more than a part of you in the loss of another, the earthly parting that, when it finally comes, leaves you totally unprepared.... Only you know that you would have chosen almost any other cross if you could have been spared this crushing blow, this "blessed release" of the beloved presence, for you have not yet come to realize that the response it has created in you is the loved one's greatest gift, the gift of a total relationship *out* of the bitter loss.

The exuberant fox terrier who once jumped madly up and down making it impossible to be patted now lies like a placid Labrador hardly daring to move while being stroked.

If we knew how dearly we were loved we would die of it. And because I was no longer afraid of the pain involved, somewhere in between my love for Jack and people was the beginning of my whole-hearted turning to the God of my heart.

But to allow the full miracle to begin happening the suffering was so acute that there are no words to describe it. It is only in the confrontation of the Terrible, my friend Irene wrote from India, that the inner eye opens and spiritual endeavor finds its fulfillment.

It has now become so difficult to write that I sit looking at all the scribbled paper around me with something bordering on despair. How can I ever make sense of it ...? Put order into it ...? Make it a sequence ...? How can I put into words something which doesn't translate? Something without a vocabulary?

It is very easy to mouth words about being "born again," words about joy and humility and suffering, prayer and surrender. Equally easy for me to think arrogantly: You haven't got a clue what you're talking about—you don't even know what these words mean. *Do you*?

Maybe you do know what *brokenness*

means. Maybe you have grieved at the waste in human life; the flowers for the wasted, funeral ones coming too late. Maybe you have been humbled to the roots of your being. Humility does not come easily, or come at all—it must be induced, and the only thing that induces humility is suffering. Maybe you have experienced yourself, then experienced God. I have only experienced myself and I cannot bear it, nor can I bear the little of God that I have experienced.

I always thought that surrender to God was tied up with love, and only love, until I discovered it was tied up with anger, hurt, frustration, bitterness, disillusionment, which, I found, are also the ingredients of love. Whether you want the purification this side of eternity or not, you will get it, if you are responsive and willing, so there is no point in flinching. The "God-loves-you-just-as-you-are" syndrome is a fairytale if you see it in the light of "God cares."

Suffering is part of your training. God is treating you as his children, the New Testament writer reassures us in the Letter to the Hebrews. To take precautions then against suffering and end up by shutting out love is plainly to *hell* oneself, in the sense of hiding oneself away from good influences and so refusing to grow.

God achieves great good among the millions who are for him because they are not against him in his hidden ministering to the world. This is in spite of our personal obstruction and seldom if ever because of our specific contribution and cooperation. And this to me is the real marvel, that however clumsy our words, however tactless our actions and misguided our motives, he can illuminate them at the right moment for someone who needs them.

I had a mountain within me, a hell within me, as we all have, and I did not know it till after it had been taken away. God can and does move mountains but what is so wonderful is the many different ways he has of doing this. My mountain was washed away by tears.

Jack had been purified by his sufferings ... made holy ... and now it was my turn. Death deepened my love for him and tears deepened my love for

God. Soon I was weeping because I saw so clearly how wide-of-the-mark my life and love had been. I was plunged into a state of continual compunction and I have not yet emerged from it.

This is the time for hurts and they come, beating like a tenderizing club on your already sensitized spirit until you are all wound. One by one your closest relationships may be undermined. Little by little you may be left in no doubt about yourself—you feel your worthlessness in your very marrow. How could God ever want or need you? He only puts up with your fumbling.

Jack was dead fewer than three months when I invited the hurts by my senseless fluttering against the bars of my cage. My closest companions were words, and these are notorious for hiding the truth. The first lesson you learn in any sort of inner distress and turmoil is that you are essentially *alone*. You can turn to God in prayer but the chances are, if you turn to a fellow human, the situation, together with your personal suffering, will be greatly compounded.

In Shakespeare's *Othello*, toward the

tragic climax, everything Desdemona says works against her because it bears a double interpretation. She is innocent but her own words convince Othello she is guilty and he murders her.

One of the most difficult human pains to endure is a jarring misreading between you and a cherished friend, or between you and someone you look up to and respect, so that the music is lost from the meeting of your souls because your wavelength, if you had one, is damaged or destroyed. There doesn't need to be a blatant accusation, just a gentle comment, maybe even prefaced by the incising words "I don't want to hurt you," and it is enough and more than enough to reduce you, numb with shock, to the lost status of a nonperson.

The most shattering and belittling words I ever in my life had to face were a stark observation about "seeking for God in prayer and finding only self." Perhaps they were harder for our priest to utter than for me to hear, but that day I knew what it was to stumble out of the sacrament of reconciliation feeling shriveled and *ugly*.

From this sort of pitiless voiding when you begin dimly to understand you have nothing anywhere apart from God, everything else being *maya*, illusion, you start to make the wonderful discovery that you are now more alive than you have ever been because of all the deadness that is being burned away.

Earthly relationships can sicken and be destroyed—and mothers have been known to murder their children—but you are now on sure ground for you have had your moment of truth and it has peeled away every vestige of pride, left you with not even a shred of it from the inexhaustible reserves of your arrogance. It is very easy at this time to lose confidence; to develop such a poor self-image that it would gnaw away at your self-respect so that nothing would be able to salvage it.

But that is not the purpose of the exercise. The self-effacing is meant to build up Jesus, to put *him* where *I* was. Saint John the Baptist says it best in the incomparable words of Saint John the Evangelist: *He must become more and more, I must become less and less.* And faith can somehow be relied upon to help you look beyond the awful pain.

The love of God is indeed carried in fragile *jars of clay*, easily withered or stunted by the inflicting of hurt—all in the name of the Christian ideal!—hurt that is too big to live down, perhaps. Fine, if the seed falls on good ground. There will be growth. But if it doesn't, who will be responsible for the loss of the little that was there before?

In our close interaction with others we will always be seen only as they think we are, seldom as we really are; we do the same, remembering people as they were in a bad situation and failing to give them credit for blossoming.

Only God's imprinted kiss reaches behind the persona we present to others where we can say anything, do anything, and yet be fully understood. Though for a while you may bitterly recall the words of a hymn:

I thank thee for the lessons taught
To lean on none save thee
That rest in any human heart
Must ne'er be sought by me

you know a fragrance is rising out of all this hurt and you are growing like a flower toward the light.

But hurt has a strange side effect. It can create closeness. Take ourselves and Jesus: We come nearer to him than the good angels who have never hurt him.

It is almost a cliché to say there is no waste with God, because anyone who has a relationship with him *knows* that as fast as you make mistakes he recycles them into a theme for praise. Now that you are on the road to learning obedience in the same way that Jesus learned it, by suffering, you are better able to see in part what your *self* is like though you will not fully know it till you experience yourself through total compassion in a *judgment* of the most positive kind. This will properly straighten you out, but in a way that the love is bigger than any pain involved.

Death must be, above all, *the* moment when you leave self-interest behind forever and focus wholly on the *Desire of the ages*. Oh yes, he loves me as I am, and receives me as I am, but he will not let me remain as I am. He will change me, like any true parent drawing out the best in me. To believe in a parent's love that does not fail to teach, because it looks to the *future* good of its offspring, is to be as near a shortcut to faith as it is possible to be, even if one didn't have the gift of faith and only believed in love—as I think nearly everyone does.

In this work of grace I took for granted the role of Jesus as Advocate until I heard a talk on the transcendental nature of God. Then I realized why we need our Savior. He puts us in touch with this otherwise too remote and perfect Being whom we may pine for and strive after but may never reach, not even in a million rounds of self-salvation through an ever-turning wheel of destiny.

He has given life meaning, he has given us hope, he has shown us a way out of death and hell, he has made us his family, called us his friends, made his inheritance ours, shared his cherished mother in the birthpangs of Calvary giving her as mother to us all, taught us to call the Unmentionable All Holy One "our Father." No one can experience his cross through physical infirmity or mental distress and not have the chance to experience his resurrection.

Suffering does not last, as one writer has said, but *having suffered* lasts forever. Like the parched earth cracking open and crying out to the rain for deliverance, we are made vulnerable and brought within reach of what was once safely on the fringes: those too demanding undercurrents of God's caring concern so well expressed by the Indian poet Tagore,

I heal you, therefore I hurt;
I love you, therefore I punish.

In fact, Jesus' sufferings, together with my own, are to me the greatest proof of the existence of another world. Else why such pains to instruct the human race?

There is a point at which everything becomes simple and there is no longer any question of choice . . .
Life's point of no return (*Markings*).

For years I had prayed: Forgive me for having so much; for being warm and well-fed and well-dressed when so many are without the barest necessities. Now suddenly I was the poorest of them all.... Still warm and well-fed and well-dressed, and even well-housed, but, worst of all, beggared in myself, "rejected" by my husband—He died on you, did he?—and rejecting myself. I felt my failure in the core of my being.

I may still smile, but smiling, like chastity, can be just a matter of habit. Something was broken in me. Dead. I didn't love myself anymore. There wasn't even any respect. I had found out all about me, my shallowness, my selfishness, my ability to destroy everything I love, to resist love, the only Love that really mattered.

As for God, if he cared anything for me it seemed at the time he was careful not to show it. (Why did I persist in believing in his love?) You have great faith, I had often been told over the years. Oh, yes! Fifteen years ago I was praying to have a conviction about one little point of the future—any point. Now

I am still praying the same prayer, and I am fool enough to believe there is nothing like loving God to love him more.

Jack had found himself by accepting death and entering the state of non-corporeal life in perfect peace. For me it was reversed. I had to accept life ... in all its turmoil and turbulence. I had to learn to give God every fear, every anxiety, all my wordless sorrows, all my ever-breaking hopes—not just speak the offering but *experience* it ... live it.

I had to learn to live without any affirmation as to whether my life was taking the right course; as to whether it meant anything to him, or to others; so that I wait ... wait ... and continually wait ... in my heart.

I had to learn to accept that while affection is a basic need of our nature and we have a right to love and be loved, I have been continually deprived of anyone to call my own so that all the love that surrounded me could never be possessed. In fact, whenever I have been particularly happy, something happens to remind me of "the sting of things too sweet." Yet I believe that Love will never cheat me in the end.

What I didn't realize was that God was slowly bringing me to the full and utter yielding up of myself to him, pet theories, favorite hangups, and all. *Where* I was going was not important. God was *everywhere*. Even *how* didn't matter, or *what*, or *when*, or *why*. Only *now*.

Detachment doesn't mean not to hurt, or even not to protest. But if you protest, your protest may be heard ... granted ... and you may regret it. To love God truly is not to interfere with his loving of you, and this is also the purest form of self-love there could be.

For a long time I was slow to learn all this, then suddenly I developed wings. I was in the high valley of tranquillity. I did not know till then that I could build a bridge, or climb a mountain, or break down a wall, or write a book.

This did not happen by following the path of complete self-denial such as the Christian saints and holy gurus have followed, but in a way most suited to my own gifts and personality, my spontaneity, my ability to respond to others, and therefore to God. I enjoy bringing people together and am always happy when friendship develops. One day this was bound to transfer to the Friend of friends.

How did it happen? Well . . . I knew God had to be *first*, but *how*? The answer was there at the back of my mind and had been for years, but I took no notice of the promptings. Outside of a religious vocation which I knew I did not have, where could I find that missing dimension that would make me know the search was over? I knew the answer, as I have already told you: God wanted my time.

Once, years ago, a person said to me: There is absolutely nothing in life we can be sure of, and my adolescent response was immediate: Oh yes, there is! One day we will both die.

Nothing profound in that, but the *one day* is the key issue. Time. The more I had, the more I wasted it.

ONE DAY I would read the Bible from cover to cover.

ONE DAY I would write a book.

ONE DAY I would set procrastination aside and do all the things I knew I had to do before my body was discarded like a crumpled envelope and my eternal self propelled beyond the bounds of no return.

If God had not intervened to remind me our time on earth must end, I might still be protesting love to him while at the same time ignoring the burning need to spend time daily in prayer over and above Mass and the sacraments; holding back from the nagging invitation to a closer walk with God, and yet continuing to hanker after him.

Now only God can interpret such a combination of sloth, goodwill and longing lying just below the surface of awareness. People might be emphatic that they neither want nor need God, but God looking into their hearts knows better.

Looking into mine he knew that my thoughts and words about him were only a substitute; good in themselves but not me. And it was *me* he wanted. But I only came to that idea after Jack was dead. Then suddenly I found myself with all the time in the world, and no excuse for not returning some of it to God.

Now Jack's death was not a punishment and you must not think that. Did God directly will him to die of cancer? Does he will the taking shape of our fears—am I to be buried alive? *Of course not.*

It is the hopes and dreams of his child, not its fears, that a father helps to bring to fulfillment. The fear and pain, if there, are only incidental. I might persist in saying: I don't want to learn how to swim, I would rather be rescued. But I will not be spared the equivalent spiritual plunge, that chance to learn.

God knew when we married that the cancer cells in Jack's blood would one day take over, but look at the way he worked it. Both Jack and I would come to our full, mature spiritual stature only because of this short, precious time together. Perfect, isn't it. No waste at all.

Only those who have recognized in their own lives the precision timing of dovetailing events, the amazing inexplicable coincidence, the incredible matching of mutual needs, can really say about no waste with God, *now I know*.

God brought good out of it for both Jack and me and each of us was given through the other what without each other we would never have had. And we know that all that happens to us is working for our good if we love God and are fitting into his plans.

Jack would have gone to God with full confidence just as he was, but when he decided to enter the full sacramental life of the Catholic church he was learning the discipline of letting go, like Saint Paul after his experience on the road to Damascus.

Until you are able to set aside the things of which you are most proud in human terms, you will never be able to say: You, Lord, not I. Because of Christ I have come to consider all these advantages as disadvantages. . . .

Jack was definitely searching, so Hans said. When they first came out to New Zealand they went to many church meetings of various Protestant denominations, but in the end he gave up, either because he didn't fit in or because Hans lost interest and couldn't be persuaded to accompany him any longer.

When I first met him he was not an affiliated member of any religious organization though he found security in clinging to a label: I was born a Presbyterian, I will die a Presbyterian.

Once, looking at his black brows and sideburns, I couldn't resist teasing that his pure Protestant stock might have been infiltrated by a trail of Spaniards, and this made Jack reiterate assertively that he was a "True Catholic" (of the Reformed stock)—in no way a spurious pro-test-ant. Universal, that's me! he proclaimed proudly.

That Jack ended up in that part of the Body of Christ he eventually chose is to me a classic example of the Lord's sense of humor. Life turns some strange ironical little corners, doesn't it, my darling. Universal, that's you.

So, ten days before his death, Jack let Jack out of his life and let Jesus enter through faith, on his own terms, whatever those terms were *for Jack*.

Gone were the pride of ego and dulling earthly values. Now there was only the reality of things hidden since the foundation of the world. And two days before his death he stood to receive the body and the blood after faith had been given to him at his own request. This was his final act of surrender—the laying to rest of all his previous doubts concerning the Real Presence. I did not know then the power of the visioning prayer, the only one I was led to pray for him, for I always pictured him as receiving holy communion.

Whether it is the breaking free from a lifeless bind or the accepting "like a lamb" of an array of homeopathic pills from the hand of your religious superior when you are an allopathic doctor and can be "struck off the medical rolls" for even associating with a homeopath, this kind of "conversion" has nothing to do with conventional religion, or with the morality of the "test" you are put to. It makes sense only to the Lord and you. Without it you cannot experience God and speak your faith like Thomas once his doubt had gone. You cannot talk of doing his will, or believe you are full of his Spirit, or know by faith that your sorrow will be turned into joy.

The pith of the story is that there must be a point of self-surrender for each one, and only each person knows what the submitted *my will* is. All right, God ... *you win*. What more can I say? I am empty now. To the bloody dregs.

Like Naboth I have lost my most prized possession, I have been hurt in my deepest relationships, You have permitted me to feel I am not worthy of the company of another human being so that I even thank you I married late and have no children, ironically repeating those ironical words of scripture pronouncing happy the wombs that have never borne, the breasts that have never nursed.

Why then like the three apostles have I seen his glory—the beauty Jesus has created out of two ordinary lives? Why do I look beyond this Calvary of earth and death to the being of sweetness and light who will one day be drawn through golden curtains into eternal mysteries?

You cannot fear a God you have learned to love as a father, and learned to love the hard way—there is no easy way of love.

. . . Whoever listens to my words, and believes in the one who sent me, has eternal life; without being brought to judgment he has passed from death to life (John 5:24).

Jesus' own lips have told me there was no judgment for my Jack.

But this is for him, for Jack—what about *me*? Still I didn't understand, I plunged into preoccupation again, the course, the course. For the rest of the time I was working on this book and *it* had top priority, not God. There was no unifying theme, however, and I knew something was missing but the harder I worked the more it eluded me.

That something was God. How could I have known that the Lord of the Universe was paying court to me, saturating me with emptiness, making everything hollow, crowding out every voice but his, drowning my human tears with the tears of his own longing for all his children and for me his child?

Many a person has opened to the one who stands *outside* the door knocking, who will take no notice of the deeper knocking within the closeness of home and family. Like Martha I hadn't been listening.

Now there is no escape from the Hound of Heaven and "that Voice is round me like a bursting sea...." My choices have fallen one by one like trees uprooted by the gale. God, if you weren't so loving a father, you know what I would call you!

It was all a matter of visuals and all bound up with reassurance. To convince God, and myself, that he really was first in my life, I would have to give him proof positive: the first and best portion of my day. The whole universe would then behold it and all doubt about his "place" in my life would be resolved. Though my fingers might be itching to get to the typewriter, I would first sit down and enjoy a quiet time with God. It was a very simple resolution but making it changed my life as well as my book, and only then was I put together after the tearing apart. Within the same framework, form and content, he lifted my book right up on to another plane; he gave it a theme and supplied the missing dimension.

Another wonderful reality shone out. None of my effort was wasted, not one sheet of all the reams I plowed through, because each time I was able to build on what I had done before. I could see it growing and taking shape before my eyes, miraculously incorporating a scribble here, a sentence there, a line ten pages before, a half-expressed thought that now was ready for the footlights. As with the course, my engrams worked on it all night and in the morning I was away like the wind. But creativity, I was to discover, does not so much lie in the first outpouring as in the intervals of tightening, strengthening and assembling.

I have never understood till now what an arrangement could do to a musical score, or the difference that could be made to a piece of music by the superimposing of a melody, as in the case of the Bach-Gounod *Ave Maria* in which Charles Gounod left the Bach prelude intact, note for note, but masterfully worked in his own exquisite tune. Arrangement and theme infuse newness, in fact, re-create a work.

I suppose every person dedicated to a project experiences this, the very concrete reward of labor. But to me it signified much more. It signified I had put the book in its proper place and life in its true perspective. This one simple resolution to make time every day for meditation and prayer became my *point of no return*. But prayer itself can be too close to agony, hurting as much as it heals.

Thank you for the helplessness that makes me like a little child. For the door to heaven, as someone reminded me holding his hand out just two feet above the ground, is only high enough for a child to enter. Not even a beggar can enter on hands and knees unless he parts with his miserable hoard, unless he gratefully acknowledges his debt to his benefactor, unless, paradoxically, he is content to beg and let go of his pitiful *all*.

Like the beggar in Tagore's poem, I have so far given you only one grain of

rice from my bowl—and it has taken me
half my life to part with it.

Take oh take—has now become
    my cry.
Shatter all from this beggar's bowl;
put out this lamp of the importu-
    nate watcher;
hold my hands,
raise me from the still-gathering
    heap of your gifts into the bare
    infinity of your uncrowded
    presence.
        Gitanjali (Song Offerings)

7

Inner Fitness through Prayer

They who are near to me do not
    know
that You are nearer to me than
    they are.
They who speak to me do not know
that my heart is full with Your
    unspoken words.
They who crowd in my path do not
    know
I am walking alone with You.
They who love me do not know
that their love brings You to my
    heart.

Author Unknown[1]

DURING those initial long months of waiting, life passed in slow motion with perpetual close-ups of the events of the past year: first the awful discovery, then the constant ringing of the telephone till one night when I still hadn't had lunch and I felt like an automatic recording machine repeating and repeating the same information, the last caller "capped" all my frustration and exhaustion and I burst into tears on the line; then the hospitals, the get-well cards, the false hopes, the inevitable end.

The sunlight still splashed into the dining room like a bucket of sunbeams some angel had overturned, still touched and haloed Jack's picture on the mantelpiece and I still avoided meeting his eyes. How could he look so happy when I was so sad?

The desire to write about him was already born and I began in February, four months after his death and before I started working on the course. The odd thing was that all I could write about was the humorous bits, and those first 60 pages did more than run away from the pain; they also betrayed the depth of our spiritual experience because what I was writing was shallow, and I knew it. In essence then the last chapters were written first, but I discarded the attempt and did not try to write again till June of the following year, about 20 months after his death.

I remember the day I found one of his hairs. It was so unexpected it had the impact of a letter—I cried for hours. It reminded me later of what one of the local funeral directors had said about the grieving process being triggered by something very insignificant in itself, in his case his tears for his father were released at the sight of the empty shoes.

Whole pictures were now present to me as I held the precious relic . . . Jack sitting on the sun porch at the back of the house enveloped in a sheet (under protest, mind you—pretended of course—because it put him so completely at my mercy) while I made a great business of trimming his sideburns and hair. He always made a point of making fun of the result, but he slyly continued to accept my unpaid services thereby making colossal savings toward tobacco and beer.

All my devotion was taken for granted in the most infuriatingly casual manner as if it was his by right (and it was) and the less said about it the better. He got away with murder just by ritually stamping his feet, each foot once, at the same time murmuring something that sounded like *eh-hay* (conveying pleased satisfaction), and the gesture was so endearing I had to feign anger to make sure he didn't get his own way too often!

Now Jack is parked at the school gate, pleased as punch to be saving me that seven-minute trudge home. His Holden station wagon is allergic to me and once too often has threatened me with electrocution, so, with impeccably continental courtesy, he always lets me in and out of the car.

Wonder how long *that* will last? the neighbors laugh in disbelief. He smiles indulgently every time I jerk my arm away and screw my face up, and I know he isn't convinced. . . .

Then one day I am completely vindicated. We are going to pick up some hardware and we are both wearing synthetic clothes and I am holding a bunch of keys. I notice a hair on his shoulder and instinctively reach up to brush it off. We don't see the blue flash but the crackle goes right through his ear and he is visibly shaken—and that really clinches my case!

This other little hair lies soft and unresisting on my palm, almost as fine as spider's silk. No static here. Only helpless and harmless tears.

"Oh memories that bless and burn...." Some, potentially funny, tore at me and if he had lived we would have been able to laugh over them as so many spouses do. I remember confessing to Gay, when we were over to tea at their place one evening long before we discovered Jack was ill, that I had beaten him up with a tea towel and she threw up her arms like a suffragette and exclaimed almost hysterically, *Join the club*—I hit Norman on the head with a plastic bucket once!

The husbands made appropriate sounds of domination and protest but I was dizzy with relief—hadn't Dale likewise admitted she had thrown a wine glass after Rob? I was *human* after all, not a monster as I imagined.

But Jack didn't live, and so I couldn't laugh about my female violence anymore or ever again.

For a long time I was not able to face my most painful memory, and for a long time also I have hesitated to share it here. But I feel this story would not be complete without it and so, with the pain of it as fresh as if it had happened yesterday, I set it down.

The background to it was as follows: In May there was a telephone call from Brisbane from my Australian Mum (former landlady) as she and the family were worried about Jack and wanted to know how things were. Knowing that Mum herself had just recovered from serious heart sugery I was deeply touched, but the May holidays were over—I was still teaching then, though only part-time. You're going in August, that's all there is to it, Jack informed me.

So I went to Australia for a fortnight, and neither of us knew about the tumor. It was seven weeks before his death. We had never been ones for stocking up the fridge so I didn't do it then. Jack was still very active . . . getting around in his car . . . and he knew how to take care of himself. Besides, Raewyn and Gay between them would be having him out to meals quite often. I was full of anticipation at the thought of seeing loved faces again and buying the things Jack needed, like that juice extractor. As usual when traveling I was busy matching up coordinates and paring my suitcase to the bone (still a toy as it turned out, thinking of clothes when Jack was dying).

Queensland had one of its incessant strikes and the airways were paralyzed while I was in Brisbane, but before the planes were grounded a letter came from Jack. Darling, I am missing you a lot. How are you, my love? Did you have a good trip over, my love? Because of the sweetness of it, and because I lost him so soon after, I read that letter in Brisbane and could not bring myself to read it again till the time I wrote this chapter.

The strike filled me with dread— terrifying suppositions that almost threw me into a state of panic. *I had to get back to Jack* ... even if it meant chartering an aircraft ... drowning in the Tasman.... Nothing would prevent me from getting back to Jack. But even as I made these brave resolutions I knew their futility and my powerlessness.

Then somehow an assurance so vivid of "He's got the whole world in his hands," came to me, and I was able to relax in confident faith. God had let me come. God would get me out. I had to believe that with all my heart. I had to *trust*, not so much in the face of my utter helplessness, but rather because of it. On the scheduled day my plane took off from Brisbane Airport and I felt I never wanted to see Australia again.

Jack was there to meet me, and we both broke down. At home there was a half-prepared Chinese meal on the kitchen bench that he was working on (he knew it was my favorite) and the vaccuum cleaner was conspicuously out to impress me. Oh my love.

Then I found out from Raewyn about all the headaches and vomiting. They had taken him home with them to their upstairs flat. Only recently, when I found the courage to ask the details, she told me he was so sick that the cup of tea she had left beside him· in the morning was still untouched by the time she went upstairs in the evening, and the whole day the terrible noise of drilling and repairs had pounded and reverberated through the building and he had endured it without a word of complaint.

Then it was time for me to return and that was all he could think of. Two weeks later we were given the result of the brain-scan. The rest of the story you know.

People can get in the way, even one's nearest and dearest. Perhaps Jack needed this time alone before his death. Perhaps the God who had allowed it to happen will also help me to get over it.

Darling, I didn't make you happy, I wept in those last days, weeping for the shortness of our time together and for the destruction of a beautiful man. But lifting the veil on the eyes of faith, I know I did, more than in a thousand years of mere earth living, for it was through me that you came to a heartfelt response to God in faith, quite irrespective of a set of beliefs. Your life's search for a spiritual reality matured and found completeness. And indirectly Gay was the occasion of this inner gift.

I will always be grateful for Hans' long-distance call telling me about the last walk the two brothers had in the garden before that final evening Mass. He had remarked: I am not religious myself but it seems to have done a lot for you. Yes, Jack had answered. It has brought me peace. My voice was stilled on the line and Hans apologized for having upset me. Oh Hans, can't you understand. These are tears of *joy*.

———————————

In my momentous resolution to spend time with God every day I used, for a time, a little study booklet based on scripture, which I have always loved; but the important thing was not the reading so much as letting God speak to my heart.

This became abundantly clear with my first reading. The prophet Jeremiah (38: 1–13) was left to die in a deep slushy pit without food or water. His enemies had gone to King Zedekiah and got him to consent to this barbarity. Then an unprecedented thing happened. The king's eunuch, Ebed-melech, a non-Jew, went to him and dared to protest: These men have done a wicked thing, he said. Quite unpredictably the king's conscience was smitten and he gave orders for Jeremiah to be hauled out of the pit.

Now that passage said nothing to me, not even with the notes. I tried and tried to apply it to my life but drew a complete blank. Then I decided to pray about it: What should it say to *me*, Lord? There was a lightning strike.

I was moved to ask myself the question: How can *I* help anyone, Lord? Well, I answered myself, how did Ebed-melech help Jeremiah? All he did was just have the courage to speak one word. Not anonymously and safely but face to face to a very arbitrary king who could have had him executed for it. One word, spoken disinterestedly at the right time with the right intention.

The power of words. To lift up or put down. To make or unmake. To save or destroy. And to think that God himself speaks and acts through a person, and that that person could be you or I. If I had the gift of words, like some of the masters of our day, what a feast I would create for the sickening, empty hearts of our cold and lonely world. There are other gems in this passage but none of them had the same impact for me.

Whether we are aware of it or not, whether we acknowledge it or not and attribute it to God or not, this work of love in the Holy Spirit is going on in us all the time and we are unfolding in the present on the attar of the past. Even those who have impeded it by abusing conscience or who have been totally deaf, may enter the process of beginning to see, hear and understand because of the vague noises that sooner or later get through.

Not one of us need feel as if we count for nothing, or as if our hands are tied, or as if we can't be used by God, because we can be and we are. In this technological age when machines have downgraded people into redundancy so that they find enforced leisure more difficult to cope with than work, a lot of what a friend calls *inner* fitness is needed if we are to survive spiritually. To be overwhelmed with the means of material survival, even if unequally distributed, while falling apart mentally, morally and spiritually, is the great irony of our times.

However, if it is God who has put us in the pit, the trenches, the holocaust, the Gulag, God will be there with us—he will be there with us even if our own selfishness put us there. Isaiah puts his tenderness another way:

> ... every moment I water it (his vineyard) for fear its leaves should fall; night and day I watch over it (27:3).

One day as I sat down to invite Jesus into my desolate inner wilderness, my awareness altered. I was lying on the beach in the sun—incredible imprinting for one whose feeling is for mountains and who has never known or loved the sea. I knew the time had come to make a conscious effort to step back into the sunshine by putting all negative thoughts out of my life for good. It was a year since Jack had died, and for the next two years I would wrestle with that resolution.

It is so easy to hang on to futile feelings of guilt or not to let go of real or imaginary hurts and wrongs. It is just as easy to bury one's negative feelings and simply cut them off, instead of facing up to what they teach you about yourself so that you finally come to terms with them and resolve them to your peace. Only then should one establish a cutoff point, and the same holds for grief. It is even important to make this slow painful walk through the fog on the scene where the loss occurred so there is no flight to facilitate escape.

But stepping back into the sunshine was a resolution I was meant to make and that Christmas it was confirmed by an Australian Jesuit priest in India who wrote:

I hope this Christmas has a special grace for you, one that you yourself will recognize as being meant especially for you.... I feel the real Shirley has come to life.... The Lord wants you to share your life and love ... because you now know, through experience, what love is all about, and how it transforms us.

I don't know whether I understand what love is all about, but I can certainly see it at work in myself and in those around me. A gallery of heartwarming masterpieces one cannot take in at a glance except through the eyes and hearts of all people of all time. Brought to a point of focus in Jesus, then, love has a meaning of its own. Because devotion to Jesus is devotion to love, but love that has a special flavor—hurt.

––––––––––

Inner fitness thrives under the most amazing conditions, often those of stress, because to be challenged is to confront oneself and to be forced along the difficult road toward one's full potential. I did not know it then but I was being drawn to make time for prayer, and more and more I would see its energy in action.

To begin with, quite early in my bereavement, I let my health run down atrociously—an easy enough trap to fall into in the circumstances. Having plunged remorselessly into the task of researching the course I was to give, I grudged every moment spent in the kitchen and decided to turn vegetarian. But there is more to this than nuts, seeds and dried fruit, and my guesswork left much to be desired. Within two months it was obvious something very unpleasant was happening to me.

I became ridiculously weak. I could hardly squeeze a sponge or grip a ball-point pen and press firmly enough to make an impression on the paper; on rubbish collection day I had to struggle to drag my rubbish bag to the footpath; a cake of soap felt strange in my hand; most frightening of all, a nasty big dent appeared in my left arm (which later disappeared) where a muscle seemed to have pulled away. Meanwhile my sense of time went haywire and I sat at the typewriter as if mesmerized, some days almost 14 hours at a stretch, oblivious to the fact that I was sitting at the edge of a hard chair (very bad for my legs) until I saw the varicose veins developing. On and on I plodded with my course. Then one day my left hand went dead at the typewriter. I could not strike another key.

The doctors were altogether mystified and some spinal tests were done involving electrodes—it did not occur to me to mention my unbalanced diet till after I was cured! At this stage I telephoned the Anglican priest who had invited me to run the course and told him bleakly I could not go on. That evening he came. He found me in an unheated room, the penetrating chill of the midwinter wind and wet reflecting the numbness of my spirits. I didn't mind dying ... but *paralyzed*? He stayed with me comfortingly for two hours and during that time we prayed. I could never have guessed how promptly and dramatically his prayer would be answered.

The next morning I awoke with the solution in my head: PROTEIN. I was suffering from acute protein deficiency!

Nothing I was eating gave me the equivalent of two ounces of meat I needed every day to stay healthy! Within two weeks of this revelation I was back to normal and by then I had also bought myself a proper cushion and learned to sit back on my chair.

I regret now that I held out for so many months against medication, not exactly antidrugs but anti the thought that I needed them; doing with less and less sleep as I maintained my furious pace of work, such a clear example of suppressed and diverted grief, or rather, abortive grieving because it did not lead to recovery.

Finally I started to reach into the cupboard for the pills that had already been prescribed, and slowly I was able to put the thought of other things and other people aside and gently give my loss the attention it needed for my true psychological healing to begin.

What is the use of appearing to take it well and denying the tears are underneath because they are not shed? When they *are* shed the true purpose of grieving is fulfilled, which is to get over it, not stay with it forever.

It should never be assumed a bereaved person is coping because he or she appears to cope. This is the time when support and friendship are needed most and they are often not forthcoming. Of course the person may cut this off because he or she resents pity, or imagines or senses people don't really care. Either way, acquaintances risk blame as the grieving person isn't his or her normal self. I know the feeling only too well—of not being my normal self.

Hello, how are you? Lovely day isn't it! In reality these conceal the pall of depression a grieving person is battling, not even up and down like an emotional yo-yo but simply perpetually *down*. I know that feeling also. My active death wish lasted fully three years. I don't want to live, I remember telling someone, meaning every word. Is it as bad as that? she replied, somehow putting it in perspective.

———————

Many times during that first year I

would go out to the back of the house and open my arms to the silence around me. Did Jack know that Norman had framed his painting for me, the favorite one? The day it went up behind his La-Z-Boy rocker did he know what it did to me? Did he care? The silence looked at me through uncountable bright eyes, distant to infinity, yet as near as my inmost self. I was not only *in* the sanctuary of God. *I was it.*

Perhaps you don't believe that God exists, and to try to "prove" it would be a wasted and boring exercise. You believe in love, don't you? When you see with love, you have faith. You don't have to be a theologian, or astronaut, or scientist to know that every segment of reality teems with greater reality. The more you see, the more there is to see.

Little by little my nightly communion with the universe brought me the growing gift of peace. Nature speaks a language all her own and words are not needed to understand. Those who are attuned and humble hear and respond, each in his or her own way.

When David Attenborough was interviewed on television about his superb series *Life on Earth*, he said in answer to a question:

I remain an agnostic, but what I experienced especially in the last three years was an increasing sense of awe, splendor and wonder, and awe, splendor and wonder are not scientific terms. They are spiritual terms.

In another way, on a different level, this sense of awe, splendor and wonder was conveyed to me very powerfully by a letter I received a year after Jack's death from the pen of our priest. More than anything else it helped to change my grief process into a growth process and I cannot express the charisma of it.

Indefinable, indecipherable, mystical, yet real, this mysterious "touching" power is something to be felt, but only in the soul. You cannot say it was this word or that thought, or even a fleeting meeting while looking out of inner windows on to outer things. Aside from its meaning for you alone it has no charisma in itself, but like a breeze blowing free it is there for you though you couldn't make it blow however much you wanted. It comes unbidden, unforced, all gift, like the deep that calls to the deep, drawn on by the mysterious forces of your own being and rising expressly to your soul's need.

All that is meant for you will find you.

The stars come nightly to the sky,
   The tidal wave unto the sea;
Nor time, nor space, nor deep,
     nor high,
   Can keep my own away from me.

For one passing moment this touch of the Inexpressible leaves you more satisfied than if you had won the unpossessed galaxy in a lottery. . . .
For one eternal moment the eternal Abstract touched and could be touched before it became again nothing but a will-o'-the-wisp. . . .

———————————

There is nothing in my life that could

have made me worthy of the quality of the people who have come into it, a most extravagant blessing that greatly humbles me. These are the people, religious and lay, whose self-offering will shine in the shining of the friends surrounding them in the home of God's love. They are indeed a city set on a hilltop, and there never was a time when these inspiring people failed to give me an example or to make me want to be a better person because of their regard for me.

They may not know it, but this book belongs to them just as much as it belongs to Jack, or me, or the Lord.

NOTES

1   This beautiful poem was presented to me long ago by a student. I assumed it was written by Tagore, but could not find it it the *Complete Works*. If you wrote it yourself, Chitra, I want you to know that I have treasured it all these years.

And let there be no purpose in friendship save the deepening of the spirit. And let your best be for your friend. If he must know the ebb of your tide, let him know its flood also.

> Kahlil Gibran—*The Prophet*

LOVE yer, was Jack's almost daily declaration. Whatever else was in question, our love and affection at least was never in doubt. We enhanced each other's qualities by contrast, Jack, the quiet realist, the out-and-out pacifist; Shirley, doting on occasionally spicing up a routine day—the less said about her the better! The reconciliation was always one-sided with me capitulating unconditionally.

If I knew at the beginning what "we" were quarreling about, by the end I wasn't so sure. All I would know was that I didn't care about Good Relations anymore but only about Venting My Fury. If Jack thought he understood women he must have felt more at home in the Hampton Court Maze.

But the moon is only beautiful in a night sky and water never seems so blue as in a desert oasis. Jack took me in his stride, flair for drama and all! Our loyalty was absolute and I cannot remember a single occasion when I spoke a word about him that wasn't loving, or a single instance when I wished he were anyone but himself. We never really hurt each other.

Both of us were very wide in our thinking. I could only find myself as one member of the human race. Or as one of the formless faceless beings of endless space working their hidden wonders in unrevealed mystery as quietly as the lowliest beings work on this familiar planet of ours, the microbe making wine for our tables, the earthworm forming humus for our gardens. Jack was less verbal about it but he had a deep sense of the grandeur of human history and of the development of art and culture.

You're so easy to choose a present for, I would say, and our pile of art books, gardening books and classical records winks in assent, but, as it turned out, *I* was not so fortunate. I was given Malcolm Muggeridge again and again until I had to put my foot down. Of course, to be fair, other goodies usually accompanied him and softened the blow—not that I have anything against Malcolm Muggeridge, quite the contrary, but my sneaking suspicion was that Jack was deviously cashing in on the MM books out of turn.

He was a happy person, always smiling, as his nephew's wife put it. His sunny disposition laid him wide open to teasing, and I pounced. Very often Jack didn't know whether he was being teased or not because I reveled in all the little twists that fed and filled out our developing relationship, and before we knew it our banter would subtly transpose into reality sweeping Jack out dangerously into deep water! Never was this more apparent than on the two occasions when we tried to play chess.

The chess set was a wedding present from Raewyn, beautifully carved in a padded wooden box. I brought it out with a flourish, eager to christen it. I blew imaginary specks of dust off the red baize lining of the interior of the box and carefully laid out the handsome wheat-colored pieces, just so.

I was self-taught, out of a book that is, and I forgot to revise all the rules I had forgotten. Jack's mood was expansive and unsuspecting, mine, free of any premeditated crime. What happened, in fact, took both of us by surprise.

At a suitably vulnerable moment I made a diabolical move. THERE was Jack's king, unbelievably, unmistakably, quite irresponsibly (I mean, even *I* could see it) unprotected. The temptation was too much for me and I wasn't even modest or delicate about it, or even faintly apologetic. Down I came like all the marauding hordes of reincarnated barbarians, swiftly and unceremoniously, devoid of any shred of diplomacy, without the courtesy of that one little magical word of warning: *check*! I annihilated him from the board, banished him from the room, hurled him from royal decency, from the prerogative of enthronement, into irretrievably lost honor and open shame before all the parading pawns, into the heartless disgrace of his padded box, now as doom-ridden as a condemned cell.

Jack was appalled. He was not only angry, he was hurt. You can't do that, you can't do that, he moaned as if staggered by the enormity of it, shattered by this terrible insult from his bride of only a few months.

Can't I? But I had.... It was a *fait accompli*. Jack stampeded round the room flinging his arms into the air in frustration. *Why* can't I do it?—I was almost crying with laughter. You just CAN'T! he shouted helplessly, too incoherent with shock and mortification to be able to explain.

Quickly I got out my booklet *Chess Made Easy*. Let the printed word arbitrate between us. Well . . . there it was in black and white and one of us would have to bow. It says . . . I started to read the vital rule but Jack cut me short in the tone of *to hell with it*.

I don't care what it says! *You can't touch the king*! That's what it says, I conceded magnanimously (always generous in defeat, even inglorious defeat such as this display of abysmal ignorance). *The king shall be spared the indignity of capture.* Jack was so ruffled that even this revelation didn't quiet him down, but he grudgingly forgave me when I lavished repentant kisses on him.

We made one more attempt to play, and I had made considerable efforts to brush up my knowledge since that terrible assault on him, but obviously as a partner, or rather, opponent, I was not Jack's cup of tea.

We did it again! It was no use saying it was only a game, because, to watch Jack play, you would have thought his life depended on it. How was he to know whether this was a game or for real? Being the villain of the piece that I usually am, he had at all costs to defend himself from me.

How perpetual is the silence now, my darling, now that the perpetual sparring is stilled forever.

To put the king back on the board I would gladly give my own life.

_____

Jack had virtues, great virtues, and I recognized him as a moderate man. He and his friends, Norman and Jim, never drank too much during their weekly visits to the pub, and Jack never ate too much either as I have already indicated. He also worked hard, but more than this, he loved and enjoyed his work. (I am taking no notice of Norm's shocking disloyalty when he maintains you never got to the worksite before ten, or of Hans' interpretation that you had to be self-employed because you couldn't get out of bed in the mornings!) Working for me however always made him very nervous on account of my insisting I could see where all the joins were in the wallpaper.

He was kind to animals and a wizard with children. Raewyn was four when Jack married her mother and took her over, together with two of her brothers. He never legally adopted them—the marriage was unstable. But measured by the gauge of love Jack was a father indeed. Hoop-ta? he would yell as he swung the little girl into the air while she reveled in the giddy acrobatics. Raewyn also remembers being walked around on his feet, something I remember of my own father who died when I was four and a half.

He was wonderful with his hands, she says with admiration. He made rocking cars for her and wooden toys, and on one occasion a very intricate chalet of twigs for a project she was doing at school. I was very proud of that, she recalls. As for his soft heart—we all know about *that*. As Raewyn tells it, once she was supposed to have been given a hiding. She bent over her bed and he whacked the bed and she yelled. I can just see Raewyn getting into the act and Jack aiding and abetting her.

All the same, escaping that hiding doesn't seem to have done her too much harm. She has grown up concerned, caring, sensible and considerate, and in her relationship with me she is thought-fulness itself. Never seems to put a foot wrong.

The kitchen was one place Jack stayed out of ... that weird and wonderful place of unimplemented gourmet flights of fancy that crystalized as raw spinach and mushroom salad with kibbled wheat and olives. It was a mean trick as far as I was concerned because when he was courting me he persevered even to cooking me a fine meal every weekend, that is, if we weren't dining out. So I naturally began to think of him as a plum of a suitor and which woman in her right senses would have turned him down?

I tried to tell him I was eagerly awaiting the day they invent a meal pill; I ate on the run over the kitchen sink, I ate just about everything raw. But he didn't take my fantasizing literally. He was also very shrewd. From the day he placed the golden band on my finger he became allergic to matters culinary *per se*. Entreaties didn't move him. Threatened strikes proved fruitless. If Jack made up his mind to do or not to do a thing, you couldn't budge him. Here was someone I had thought as guileless as mother's milk and he had sprung this nasty surprise on me.

To be fair (mind you, being fair doesn't come easily and Jack was always saying plaintively *That's not fair*!) I must admit he was unfailingly generous with the washing up, which I thoroughly enjoy anyway, and he patiently submitted to the rinsing routine. He appreciated my efforts with meals but when he saw the unsparing lengths to which I went if we were expecting company, he would declaim authoritatively: That's *it*. This is the *last time* we're entertaining! I never quite worked out whether this was because it pained him to see me worn to a frazzle with planning, shopping and preparing, or because he found himself unwillingly embroiled in the chaos.

My darling, it was nearly a year before I could bring myself to ask friends and the table was full again.... How well she copes, everyone thinks. Shirley is very self-sufficient, another says. You look so well, someone else beams (meaning to be complimentary). If only they knew.

More contrasting lives than Jack's and mine you could hardly have imagined. I was an only child. My half brother and sister from my widower father's first marriage were old enough to be my parents. He was 16 years older than my mother and died in an asthmatic seizure in his late fifties. She outlived him by fewer than eight years—my first close-up of cancer. Then I was looked after by my half sister who had no children. She sent me as a boarder to the local convent, and a Christian education became the success story and miracle of my life. I was then 13 years old.

Ironically, by the time we met, Jack was far more alone that I was. In the three countries in which I have lived I have always been surrounded by a sizable number of acquaintances and a coterie of friends, together with many interests, so any deep longing for a perfect life-sharing is more for overflow than for need or loneliness. The two of us were a dynamic combination of differences: he a Dutchman, now a New Zealander; I an Anglo-Indian,[1] now an

Australian. Education, religion, nationality; all were bridged by love, and horizontal space was unified in vertical time.

To the astrologers also we presented no problem! They smiled benignly as we grew bright with all the star blessings promised to a Scorpio woman and her Cancer man. Cancer . . . Latin for Crab. The ten legs of the crab insidiously probing a man's healthy organs and tissues, slowly but surely killing him. This man, my man. My Jack.

Funny how he had a Latin name too, Jacobus, translated James. And if it weren't for his avoidance of the ridiculous English habit of clipping words, he would have been Jim instead of Jack. Jim is a cunningly devised contraction designed to take the aristocratic ring out of a name like James, whereas Jack has no glory to lose. Plain unromantic Jack. Also a name in its own right as well as being a nickname for John (though one fails to see how).

Shirley, on the other hand, is quite bourgeois in origin: the name of an English bird (feathered animal), the *shirl* or *shirle*. The "ey" or "y" was added later as a diminutive, as in Janey and Harry. Amazing how useless knowledge latches on! But at least I know I am one person in a million who actually comes out tops in the battle of name versus nickname. Shirl in affection gives me my real name; Shirley, the name given at my christening. So either way I win.

But *Jack* and *Shirley* were reserved for very formal use. More particularly they signified a hint of displeasure or the onset of a quarrel, usually faked (until it escalated into reality). The exact tone of Jack's voice would determine the gravity of the situation. *Shir* . . . ley! drawled out with mock menace, head bent down and eyes turned up in preparatory bull-charge fashion, meant I was definitely going too far and had better be warned OR ELSE.

Once, to my shame, we had a genuine argument . . . about religion . . . the last thing in the world I wanted to argue about. Religion is the sublime, awe-inspiring, moving interaction between God and man and it should liberate and uplift, not bog down and make jittery. It is man and God seeking each other and is worthy or respect. Narrow attitudes always frustrate me.

I do not hold Jack guilty of intolerance but I used to get hotly belligerent over some of his inbred misconceptions about the Catholic church, though he did recognize the growth and change of attitude that had taken place.

We sat in the car and argued, somewhere in the city. I was waving my arms about, obviously furious, and my negative radio waves must have scorched the house in front of us. A man came out and stood in the doorway very placatingly, smiling and saluting us with the beer bottle in his hand and imprinting himself on my mind so that even now, over six years later, I can still picture him, bless him. What he said we didn't hear but the message he conveyed was very loud and clear: whatever it was we were arguing about, wasn't worth arguing about.

How right he was, I stood properly corrected and it never happened again.

Unfortunately scripture, man's crowning heritage, can also provide a fertile ground for contentious dispute if taken out of the context of its development over 1600 years. It is all very confusing for those who would like to come to God like a friendly puppy instead of a neurotic dog who has learned to be suspicious of every passer-by.

His spirit, the Holy Spirit, blows "like the wind in a thousand paddocks, Inside and outside the fences," as the New Zealand poet James K. Baxter so eloquently put it in his *Song to the Holy Spirit*.[2] Posturings do not bother him or the limited views of human minds that still lack understanding. He can work in any medium, blowing wherever he chooses.

There are so many ironies in life. To all appearances I was spiritually stronger than Jack because I was the Christian by commitment and he wasn't; I was the one who had access to the grace of the sacraments; I was the one who was informed, the one who prayed.

Yet *he* was the one through whom I would really become myself. Without him I would never have been able to allow God to turn me inside out and graft me to Jesus so that I was given a golden heart like the beautiful little ivy whose plainness is transformed when it receives this additional beauty mark. I needed Jack, and the cross that crucified us both, to help me to give God the love I wanted to give him but didn't seem to know how to give.

One aspect of Jack's life I have not yet touched upon: Jack the fisherman! Gay has given me a glimpse of the pre-Shirley days when Jack, Norman and Jim went off in pursuit of that sparkling elusive creature, the trout. As the season approached, excitement and expectation would reach fever pitch. They would get up very early and the house (Gay's) would fill with the aroma of freshly fried eggs and sizzling bacon. Over steaming cups of tea they would sit and watch the dawn filter across the sky, then they were off in Jack's white Holden, laden with all their gear and Gay's apple pie and other delectables.

It was indirectly as a result of one of these fishing trips that I met Jack—but that's another story. To it and to the development of our relationship I will devote a whole chapter.

NOTES
1 The term "Anglo-Indian" refers to: 1) British or Europeans who settled in India for at least a generation; 2) children born to them while resident in India; or 3) offspring of mixed blood, sometimes called Eurasian.
2 Oxford University Press

9

To Illumine and Adorn

Death is not the snuffing out of a candle.

It is the putting out of a lantern because the dawn has come.

Old Chinese Proverb
(also attributed to Tagore)

THERE is something awe-inspiring about the sheer mass of people living on our planet today, all collectively thinking, feeling and acting as the weight of their concerted striving carries them forward in that specific historical movement that makes time what it is: *change*.

Generations have trod,
    have trod, have trod.

But these are not just people *en masse*. These are individuals, each with a particular brand of uniqueness, composite of a personal story of love, hope, courage, pain. Laughter too, unduplicatable, rising from the tears.

Jack and Shirley, two of the 20th century's four billion, separated by different hemispheres: east and west, north and south. Scientifically, what were our chances of meeting (even supposing that an ape *could* type a Shakespeare sonnet accidentally)? I wonder.

I look back over our lives, now that it is all over, and I am filled with admiration at the finely tuned intricate web of forces slowly but surely bringing us together. That blind and meaningless void called *chance* has no place in anything that happened to us. Just beyond our meeting place at the flux of the oceans was something neither of us bargained for . . . the suffering was hidden from us so we wouldn't miss out on the love.

Yet if I could choose the circumstances of my life, not in a million years would I wish to unlive this my most powerful experience. It has been said that love must always have something more to it or love is a bankrupt. And if it weren't for that more and more to love, that tiny ray of glory-light festooning the far-flung invisible worlds beckoning our earthly love toward a heavenly one, how unbearable our accumulated grief would be.

There are so many links in the chain to invest with meaning, so many loose ends to draw together, so many patterns in the weave to highlight.... Images of the past come back to me wearing the colors of shot silk according as I turn them this way and that: now peacock blue ... now crimson ... emerald green ... royal purple ... sunset pink....

I gave the impression of being the world's most confirmed bachelor girl but I always knew I would marry, though only in my own time and never merely for the sake of marrying. The search for the Holy Grail. The belief that marriage was worth waiting for and that it can be "made in heaven"; that I didn't need to find the right man—he would find me.

Why aren't you married? was the question that recurred with boring inevitability everywhere (you see, people are all tinted with the same brush), while, to those who did not know me, my single status was wide open to speculation.

To be 40 and to be unmarried is like being Methuselah's maiden aunt, a psychological aberration surely, to be regarded with suspicion. If you marry you cannot be either a misanthrope or a misogamist! You are more socially acceptable; far less conspicuous. Above all you are protected from constant misinterpretation.

One's chosen state of life has something of mystery in it, so too one's choice of this person instead of that person, if one does marry.

In his Epilogue to *Pygmalion* George Bernard Shaw gives a brilliant analysis of why Eliza Doolittle married Freddy Eynsford Hill and not Professor Higgins, and for me the pith of the essay lies in Shaw's idealism. He quotes Landor's remarks: To those who have the greatest power of loving, love is a secondary affair.

Happiness and fulfillment do not necessarily come from a sexual partnership—husband and wife, boyfriend and girlfriend (and if I don't, then what's wrong with me?)—but from *pursuit*; of goals, of ideals, of knowledge, of achievement. Deep down and paramount is also the all-encompassing search for love, not only as a concept, but as a person, or Person.

But for the great majority this kind of love is learned in marriage—I know for me it was. To be "in love" isn't always to know love by definition: the love that is stronger than death, the love that lays down its life for another, that has tender regard, shows compassion, forgives. Being a deeply emotional state it can be self-destructive in its intensity, carrying one to the point of almost dying of it so that the only relief would be the destruction of the destroying love.

Once in a lifetime only may one hear words such as: I love you, so much, so much, my very restraint is the greatest compliment I could pay you. (And you disallow the making of "tender and beautiful love" because another stands in the way and the finality of it leaves you both without hope.) Not many people, perhaps, marry the person they first loved or really loved as "few of us marry where our hearts lie."

But love, so different from the grand passion, is total commitment. However ordinary and unromantic it may appear, it is never trite or commonplace. It doesn't flaunt itself or make demands and it gives as much as it takes. It is real because founded on truth. It is built to last. It can be quietly heroic. Like Cyrano de Bergerac's love for the beautiful Roxane it is a case of "I love thee not *any* more, but *ever* more and more" (Edmund Rostand's play read in translation).

To learn in this school of a lasting relationship is not easy, but I would far rather choose it and have love grow in depth and intensity, suffusing all other relationships, than briefly enjoy the object of my adoration and then find myself at a dead end—and see love die.

Love is not made to order. Dante

was only nine when he fell in love at first sight for the first and last time and never ceased to see Beatrice in his soul, long after her marriage to another and till the day he died 31 years after her death. But love can be trained to grow, the final mystery even more mysterious than the spontaneous state of being in love. However, sadly, one lover invariably dies first and, even sadder, love itself could die.

It was not the fear of such a total commitment with all the implications and the risk of failure that led to my breaking off an understanding in India twice and an engagement in Australia. With love on the pedestal on which I had placed it the words I had once heard in a film seemed to fit me perfectly: Some people are born to be alone.

And then destiny led me to New Zealand and to Jack.

And he then had fewer than four years to live.

Outwardly I may seem to be back to square one, but inwardly? An explosion.

Not one of us can say we are neglected by the powers that be. All we could possibly need to beg the bud to become a flower is given to us in the circumstances of our lives, just as they are. We might think we know better but we don't. He will see to it we are given, like the rich young man in the synoptic gospels, the opportunity to rectify the one thing we *lack*—something perhaps, we have to give up; something we might have to take to ourselves—because, paradoxically, this, and not our plenty, is the price of the pearl of great value.

The development of my friendship with Jack is a story in itself but I will just say that he told me he began to hope when on a picnic for only us two I offered him a bite of my sandwich!

What does he say about me? I quizzed Gay on one occasion. Well,—but don't ever tell him I told you (I promised)—he says: Shirley is like a beautiful work of art that I have only seen at a distance and not yet begun to touch. The poetry of it. I started to melt like butter.

I remembered the words of the wise and holy old Punjabi woman who was letting me a flat in New Delhi: If God wants you to marry he will bring the man to your doorstep, and if he doesn't, you can roam the world and you will never find him.

It sounds very fatalistic, yet it expresses a deep truth. If you are led by faith then you can only travel the way of faith. God had in fact done exactly what she said: brought the man to my doorstep. One is always free to plot the course of one's life by following one's own inclination and judgment, but a gentle nudge or unmistakable push, or even an inexplicable seemingly irrational conviction implanted in one's mind and taking root, may propel one into a particular orbit where for that person the distant glory lies.

And yet exactly one week before our wedding I was handing Jack back the ring ... giving him all the resons why I couldn't marry him. I don't even think I love you, I finished off. And very quietly, very gently, he answered, I think you do.

To this day I don't know why those words of his carried so much conviction for me, but somehow they did. *Jack* knew I loved him, and that was enough for me.

If I had known what was in store, would I have been willing to accept a first-class ticket to Calvary? Knowing myself I would without doubt have put love before all other considerations, but ... it is a very loving Wisdom that conceals our future from us so we can better cooperate in our own improvement and development. My sense of loss is so much bound up with my finding of Jack that this book would be incomplete without this chapter.

———————

Mid-January and goodbye to Australia's eastern states—a sun-drenched Wellington—destination Napier, New Zealand. I had resigned from my secondary position in Brisbane after four wonderful years and was now on my way to a new beginning in a country that had magnetized me on a fortnight's visit. The Holy Spirit was using my restlessness to create something beautiful out of my life, though as yet in the future. Only the decision was mine. The rest was his.

After the great cities of Asia and Australia, Napier looked not only empty but minuscule. A feeling of strangeness settled in together with a sense of mounting isolation and irrational homesickness for Australia. Every day I used to think I could not stand it any more. I was going BACK.

All the same, thank God I did not give Napier away. My debt to it for spiritual growth can never be repaid for it is here I had the deepest experience of my life and met the people, attitudes and circumstances that have so profoundly influenced me. And once the school year began I felt better.

In June I decided to attend some meetings of the Astronomical Society held in the Planetarium and it was arranged for one Mrs. Gay D. who lived in my area to give me transport. And that's how it all started.

Gay is blonde, bouncy and petite, full of articulate comment. When I heard they had just had their sixth child I said with crass stupidity: You must be great lovers of children. No, we are just great lovers full stop! she answered laughing. (Norman lets out one of his famous groans, a cross between a roar and a yell expressing pain, shock, disbelief, embarrassment and heightened amusement all rolled into one!)

Gradually I heard about Jack. A dark mysterious presence below the level of awareness. A dear friend, greatly loved by the children. One Christmas he presented Gay with some art equipment which precipitated a frenzy of creative activity rocketing her to immediate fame among family and friends (she later even became a recognized local artist). Norman's framing jobs for her were in themselves works of art, each perfectly complementing the painting and accentuating its beauty and meaning.

By November I knew quite a lot about Jack, his passion for art, his broken marriage, but I had not yet met him. What I did not know at the time was how much their friendship had lit up his life, and his theirs, when it began after Jack's unhappy marriage of eight years had finally ended in a second, and this time permanent, desertion. To them must go the tribute for the eventual healing of his deep hurt and the breaking down of the barriers of suspicion and impenetrable reserve that surrounded him in the presence of women.

Jack opened new doorways for Gay, just as he did for me later, the whole hitherto unexplored world of art and the old masters, only names till he made them real. To use Gay's words:

He bought books and books and more books. We talked by the hour—Art, Art, Art. The love affair had begun. It was a love affair that involved us all, Norman, the children and myself. How we all loved him. There was a place for him in our family. His every visit was hailed with delight.... We all responded to his ready smile and his endearing manner. It was a happy time. It seemed it would last forever.

Then one day I heard about this fisherman's dinner.... It happened at the start and close of the trout season, after the hard labor of replenishing their impressive array of trout flies with further alluring bits of fluff and feathers, and of oiling their reels and pulling them to pieces and putting them together again (Gay's descriptive words). Behind it were the wives, Gay and Cecilia, clearly green-eyed that their men were having all the fun out there on the river bank in their ecstatic weekend.

So the workmates, Jim, Norman and Jack, who were also best friends, had to treat the ladies to a restaurant dinner. (Later in the piece I was to query Jack about their catch because no evidence of it ever came home—he always insisted they ate it all, but who "got one" and who didn't remained a deep dark secret.) They are going to the TraveLodge.

The first time a fisherman's dinner had been engineered Jack's teenage daughter Raewyn had made up the sixth, but this time Gay is asking me to be his partner (managing to convey the impression that I will be doing them a great favor). I refused to be fooled.

Gay, I warned, I'll come, but you must understand nothing can come of it. (There was plenty of evidence of her maternal heart and I was not taken in by her kindly scheming. As a future matrimonial proposition Jack simply didn't exist for me.) I'm just not interested, I insisted ungraciously.

We went to the TraveLodge. Quite obviously I didn't exist for Jack either. And for all the attention I received I could have been wearing sackcloth instead of my pretty long-sleeved ankle-length dress with blue-green peacock tonings.

Not once did he dare to look at me, let alone address a single word to me. He was overcome with shyness and did most of his talking directly to Norman and Jim and only indirectly to us. His unusually marked accent made it difficult for me to understand anything he said, but the others, I noticed, had no such difficulty. They were perfectly attuned to him.

What a vibrant person he was—look at him in the thick of the conversation with Norm and Jim, they're rubbing sparks off one another!

In December we met again, Christmas dinner with Gay's family, and for the first time I saw Raewyn, lovely at 17 though a bit withdrawn (not surprising in a room full of people), and her blue sun dress set off her temporarily beach-burnt skin. Jack and I didn't pay much attention to each other. All I remember was a very animated presence and the repeated "Hey, Norm!" said as only Jack could say it.

On another occasion the men chauvinistically segregated themselves and played cribbage. From our inferior corner I noticed that when Jack's shyness was out of the way he was into everything: art, politics, work, fishing, religion, his native Holland, generalities, you name it. All three of the men smoked heavily though at Christmas it was Dutch cigars instead of cigarettes. (Jack would later change to a pipe and finally he would give up immediately after the X-ray result was disclosed. Norman also gave up the instant he heard about Jack. Jack used to break down every time he thought about Norman giving up on account of him. Raewyn too.)

Five months passed. In May the following year a call from Gay—one of our usual rhapsodic communications,

I thought. But no, there was something else. Will you be Jack's guest again? she finally asked, coming to the point after a long preamble. No, I said with finality. Not unless he asks me himself.

Poor darling Jack, that telephone call was an ordeal. While he stammered into the receiver I laughed—I laughed a lot in those days—of course I'll come, silly! Jack almost levitated with relief, confiding to me later he was sure I would "knock him back."

Why, my darling? Am I such a female chauvinist? I don't mind telling you now I had to come right off my pedestal so you would feel more comfortable in the presence of such a superior being!

Now that the ice was broken Jack found it easier to ring again. Would I go with him to the New Zealand Ballet? *Firebird*, I think it was. We dined out first. Alas, replete with wine and good food and cozily positioned near a wall heater, I became a Siamese cat on a velvet cushion.... The climax of *Firebird* came and went in a crescendo of swirls and pivots without penetrating my luxurious dream world. Jack's reaction was one of incredulity though he chival-rously refrained from expressing it till long afterward, then, to hear him talk, you'd think I'd gone into a *coma*.

All the same, he gave me many other chances to retrieve my self-respect as a genuine culture vulture, but was it just coincidence that our outings became a trifle more bourgeois? Picnics, drives, runs in the park, tag on the beach when we weren't collecting pebbles, dodges with imaginary UFOs on our excursions to friends in the country, even shopping together (Jack's pet hate) and, among the nicest of all, dining out.

Slowly his speech was becoming har-monious to my ear and I didn't have to say *I beg your pardon* so often. Little by little his story unraveled and it became crystal clear to me that my church would consider him a free man. Little by little also I began to see that no one could hold a candle to him for looks and charm—I was by then *very fond* of him.

But if I thought I loved Jack at the time of our marriage I had no idea of the meaning of the word *love*. I had to be consumed like a tree in a forest fire, the life-giving sap that rises against gravity to feed each leaf, bud and twig now boiling white-hot and convulsing the tree in agony. Love had to become fire with the pain now added to it so only the purest part of its being would survive.

But we are not metal for the foundry. We are flesh, blood and spirit. In being bent we can break. In being seared we can be disfigured. This would have to be a once-in-a-lifetime experience.

———————————

Happiness is . . . courting and being courted. How light-heartedly we teased each other during this wonderful floodlit time. I wouldn't have been me if I had let him forget the time he came to pick me up on the occasion of our fourth meeting. Gay was having people to dinner and she sent him round to fetch me as she was running late (by then I was more than a little suspicious of being included in invitations that included Jack).

He was not used to this diplomatic, responsible role and he coped by being, or appearing, as unconcerned as possible. If he was nervous it didn't show. What did show was that he was casual to a degree. I will have nothing more to do with him, Gay, I complained into her cream telephone the next day, he didn't even open the car door for me—just got out and stood there with his hands in his pockets *whistling*—and I was all dressed up for the evening too! I wailed it in the outraged tone of JUST THINK OF IT, imputing to Gay her fair share of the responsibility. She made reassuring amorphous excuses for Jack's manners but I was not appeased. We obviously viewed him through different eyes.

Jack went to great lengths to repair the damage once he discovered my personal opinion of his gracelessness—he may still whistle and have his hands in his pockets, but he opens the door! I don't think it hurt too much because of the way he got kissed for it. I always lit up when he did things for me. He made me feel beautiful.

Eventually talking about marriage just happened. We applied for permission through our priest and it came in little more than a month. For those who are wondering how and why, the facts of the case are simple and straightforward. Jack's ex-wife had a previous marriage regarded by the church as binding; her subsequent civil marriage to Jack if invalid for her was equally so for him.

At the time he and I married he had been single for four years. But first we had a three-month engagement and Jack bought me a diamond ring (he wasn't going to get away with not giving me one). He swears I took it out of the box to try it on and simply KEPT IT ON so he never even had a chance to present it. (Fancy that! I was always doing him out of his little act, if he is to be believed, which I *doubt*.)

My second Christmas in New Zealand. So happy. So happy. Our wedding was three months away and in the meantime I was getting to know Raewyn. Little did she and I know how close we were to heartbreak. Our loved one was soon to be plucked from our midst and no prayer of ours would hold him back.

Uppermost in my mind are three pictures of Jack which stood out at this time like little spring buds on a hibernating tree. In September, three months before we became engaged, Jack took me up north by car to meet Maartje, Paul and their families. We returned via the east coast (Gisborne). It was pouring like a giant watering can that had lost its spray nozzle and every hotel and motel was booked out to visiting rugby teams and their fans. Even the motor camp was full. We would just have to sleep in the car.

The sky was uniform with black nimbus cloud. My first night under the stars and I wouldn't even see them; might even miss the odd UFO materializing for my benefit. I might finger my binoculars but I would not see even a pinpoint of light from Orion's fiery Betelgeuse, so hot that a five-cent piece dropped flaming from it onto New Zealand would reduce us to ash in one minute. No Southern Cross. No rising Phosphor. Not even the ghost of an Aurora Australis. The heavens were closed to me. I got niggling with Jack. *He* settled himself on the back seat and managed to drop off. I sat up all night like a martyr.

Then it began ... the snoring. It began at crescendo, suddenly cracking the rain-roar. I don't know if it was his cramped position, or whether perhaps the wound-up windows magnified it, but I had never heard anything like it *in my life*. The pitch, the tones, the reverberations, the grunts—surely this isn't *Jack*.

By morning I was thanking my (invisible) lucky stars I had found him out in time. Marriage with someone who could put on such a concert was OUT OF THE QUESTION. (To be fair I must admit this was the only time he ever snored.)

The other picture was of Jack getting out of the car later on the same journey to replace a flat tire. I waited for a *bloody* but it didn't come. Surely there'd be a *damn*—at least a damn? There wasn't. Not even a single negative comment. He set to work *whistling*.

I was so impressed I forgot about all the snoring. (Bloodies were uttered during our marriage but unfortunately they came from me, mainly for dramatic effect to lend a touch of choler when Jack was being too phlegmatic!) Right now however Jack is soaring in my opinion poll.

Then there was the third memory of him, the most endearing one. A party of Australian secondary students and two Sisters would be touring New Zealand during the holidays and the nearest they could get to Napier was Rotorua. I decided to go by bus to meet them. I will take you, Jack offered. This was the time I really began to warm toward him. He was putting himself out for me and it would be difficult not to appreciate him. He was making himself indispensable!

After this I knew I wanted to marry Jack, though there was that brief time of uncertainty one week before the wedding that I have already told you about. Nothing unique really about this last minute indecision, this butterflies-in-the-stomach, especially for the bride. All my fears were now laid to rest. I was waking to the full radiance of a moon that, with the whole sky to wander in, had chosen *my* little area of window to illumine and adorn.

It was great fun getting mentally adjusted to my future new name and I was, I must admit, secretly relieved to be getting rid of my surname *Freese* (also Dutch), never pronounced properly or spelled correctly. It was difficult to live down being frozen up with a *z*, especially when a young man from under whose hand I had withdrawn mine on our first (and last) date, had written me off to his friend with a disdainful "FreeZe by name, freeZe by nature!" Etymological devolutions dogged me: *Freeth*, *Freesie*. I should have fared better in New Zealand but several people insisted I was *Friis*. No use trying to politely let them know. They knew better. So, good riddance, name.

It didn't take me long to discover that *Koers* had the same hazards, though without any sinister implications. I told my students it was pronounced *Korsh* in a vain effort to sound it the way Jack did. Ali, Paul's wife, wouldn't have it. It's plain *Kors* she said. Gay and Norman had been used to saying *Kers*—which I kept visualizing as *Curs*! Most people compromised by saying *Ko-ers*.

On Lady Day, March 25, the Annunciation of the Lord, I chose to take on my new identity. It celebrates the Angel Gabriel's mind-blowing deputation to a very youthful Mary: Hail, O favored one, the Lord is with you . . . (which the *Living Bible Paraphrased* renders exquisitely as: "Congratulations, favored Lady!"). Holy Mary, Mother of God, what a price she would have to pay. She is only a teenager, younger than the ones I used to teach—what does she know?

Could any mother bring a child into the world who would have a future like her Son's? You don't have to be grown-up to have faith, wisdom, or love. To say yes to the Holy Spirit—as Mary, the Lord's handmaid, did—in whatever way is right and fitting for you, is to have the vibrant, compassionate, wonderful Jesus grow within you making the dark little room of your own annunciation as wide as the waiting world. Humanity, heir to the universe, has now in Mary reached the ultimate. And of this kingdom, God's and man's, there will be no end.

Till death do us part. I, Shirley, take you, Jacobus, to be my husband. I have vowed to be faithful, to love unconditionally.

I have given my heart, my life, my whole self, to another human being. One whom I have freely chosen, whom I will love wholeheartedly and never take love back. One through whom a higher purpose will be mysteriously accomplished in both of us.

But I did not understand this till after it was all over.

10

The Gift of Jack

And God shall wipe away all tears from the eyes of his people. Never again shall they weep for sorrow, never again shall they cry of pain, because sorrow, pain and death shall be taken away from them.

Revelation 21:4

THE handling of the sympathy mail is one of the most demanding tasks facing a bereaved person. Whereas the funeral director manages everything connected with the interment service, and friends and church members come forward to help so that no worry attaches to the stricken family or person, the letters that pour in are your responsibility alone. How you will deal with them is entirely up to you.

Even if you put a thank-you notice in the papers to spare yourself the formidable and harrowing business of personal acknowledgment, there is still the matter of informing relations and friends away from the scene for whom some detail must follow the starkness of the telegram or cable. But in spite of the magnitude of the task, I would not have wanted to be without this wonderful means of support. People create consummate little gems out of their love, friendship and self-offering, and their letters are a precious spiritual possession. Here are a few examples.

From Irene in India came these powerful words:

The message of life for everyone of us is to be able to put death in its right place and know that I AM THE RESURRECTION AND THE LIFE. Then we see that the physical body is, after all, only a fraction of life

284

itself. It is very important, it is very real as far as it goes, but it is only the life of the spirit, the life of love and surrender to love, that is really real. But this is something we have to learn through bitter and painful experience.

And from Leila, words that were very consoling because they made me feel so loved and wanted. Later, writing of my proposed book, she said:

> ... it will be a creation of love and pain, like a pearl.

Amiti, a convert from Hinduism and a published poet in her own right, wrote from England:

> Do you ever read Teilhard de Chardin? I find his writing full of a richness and vitality and positive thinking— even sickness and death and dying he transforms into life because the principle is Christ. . . . To be a Christian is to be constantly renewed—to let the Holy Spirit renew us so that we may change the face of the earth.

One young Dutch woman whom Jack and I had met on our tour of Paris and who later visited us here in New Zealand with her husband, labored over a letter in English which was "not so best" as she put it, to remind me that God tempers the wind to the shorn lamb. I wept over that letter and its news that both her husband and father had given up smoking on account of Jack.

The late Father Robert Antoine of the Society of Jesus wrote from Calcutta:

> Jack is gone and you have shared with all your friends the experience which brought your life to a peak.... Our love for you and Jack is weak and feeble, compared with the love by which God has united both of you in the embrace of life and death.... Looking back at the itinerary which your life followed, I see everything unified and made significant in the climax of the last weeks of Jack's earthly life.... How God prepared you for the supreme gift of yourself is something which passes human understanding.... I know and I feel

that pity would be the most jarring response to your message.

There were letters expressing gratitude that I should have been the one to share those final years with Jack, letters telling me about the slide pictures of us, about how well and happy we looked, about the vivid memories of our visit, about how we had reached a goal in less than three years, about how much we were loved, about the shock it was.

I cannot understand it but you both look *so happy*, Jack's sister Maske wrote from England, referring to a photograph of Jack and me standing under the profusion of manuka blossoms three months before the end. Was it an accident that an unexpected visitor should have requested this pose and that it, more than any other picture, best expresses our spirit?

Some letters made me feel very humble, like the one that said I had brought out the best in Jack. Oh no. It was the other way around. And then the dear letter from Leila's brother that expressed what bordered on anger that "purity and innocence should suffer so much." Believe it or not, this was the unkindest cut of all! No one of course, is pure or innocent, only Jesus and Mary—and look how they suffered.

Another, this time openly angry, letter from a dear Australian friend referred to the controversy raging in West Germany about cancer, and to a certain Professor H. who had created the biggest stir (possibly ever in medical history) by:

> accusing doctors of operating, treating etc., cancer patients when a) there is no cure possible anyway, b) when there is insufficient evidence that it is actually cancer, c) when there is insufficient evidence for the dangerous outcome for the cancer. He accuses doctors of being motivated purely for the financial and experimental aspects. Case histories from these articles are hair raising. Every day the papers have articles from this professor and replies by other experts. Every day I have been reading them and now your letter comes. . . .

Financially, Jack's treatment cost us

nothing and he received the best. About the "experimental" aspect of it I hesitate to comment. I do know he was subjected to a very large number of X-rays, running into hundreds, and that with his permission many student doctors were brought in to see him. I would like to be noble and say I am glad he did not suffer in vain but my gut feeling is that the severity of the treatment undermined his stamina and shortened his life. At least now I can say it without bitterness.

In the same letter this friend goes on to say:

Many of the great writers of the world could do their best when face to face with tragedy, passion, illness, etc. I feel you have the capacity to write something really deep and wonderful. Please consider it.

You'll never know how much this book owes to your encouragement—but may the great writers also consider pardoning the inclusion of Shirley in the same breath with them!

Sympathy letters help the grieving

process along, nearly every one striking a chord somewhere. Tears follow, but seldom come alone. They release love. They turn into the gift of prayer. They heal.

The web of concern spun round you gives a sense of direction, and above all, it comforts. One letter that comforted me greatly came from a Cistercian monk who was in Wellington Hospital at the same time as Jack and whose pajamas I used to launder and iron every day with his.

> You seemed so devoted to one another. Jack was so proud of you and wanted so much that I would meet you....

Jack was so proud of me, he said. I, who went down to the pit in self-rejection and took upon my breaking shoulders the whole responsibility for the awful loss.... Perhaps one day I will believe it—when there is no longer any need for comforting. This book is shouting how proud I am of *him*.

And there is one letter I cannot pass

over because it so perfectly combines the mirth and melancholy of things.

There's not a day goes by when I have not been thinking of you—today I picked a bunch of daisies from our garden and I recalled the giggles we had over a certain bouquet in your room!

The bouquet referred to saturated the guest room with the heavy smell—I can't say scent—of dirty socks and I was acutely embarrassed and finally confessed that I couldn't understand why my stockings were doing what they had never done before!

I entered the arena slowly and it took me well over a year. Because I know by experience how draining this labor of love is, I am now very careful when I write a condolence letter to let it be known I do not expect a reply. This removes a sense of obligation.

Inevitably a few letters jarred. Those that told me glibly "I know how you feel" when the writer had never experienced a deep loss; those that brushed aside the reality of Jack's death and immediately plunged into the writer's "news"; one that wished me joy, peace and happiness at Christmas (coming only two and a half months after the sad event) and even unrealistically suggested I cheer up and smile, the idea being that Jack had been spared further suffering by being taken away. I also reacted rather negatively to the occasional cliché such as "God loves you," as I already knew this in a way too big to bear and I didn't need to be patronized.

But I was very grateful for them all, especially the letters pointing me forward to the "new era of usefulness stemming from tragedy." It is so easy to give up and give in when one is prostrated by grief. To stay at this level would be a disaster, so anything that helps you to pick yourself up is a godsend.

Concerning the usual cards at the festive season I must admit I very much appreciated the sensitivity of those who refrained from sending me greetings, that first year particularly; but this is only my personal feeling. Others might be hurt by a change of pattern and might need to feel their friends and relations were still thinking of them.

One Christmas wish however was greatly wept over and found its way into my *Jacobus* file. It arrived hidden away in the long brown envelope containing the parish newsletter and it was a while before I opened it. Our priest said:

> May the Lord give you the strength to bear the cross he is asking you to carry.... May your tears of love purify you and help you to be grateful to God for the greatness of the gift of Jack.

The greatness of the gift of Jack. A gift too great to receive until I had learned to suffer. A gift of earth that somehow became a gift of heaven. A gift that would grow with time and one day surprise me when time was no more.

This unassuming, even diffident, man, sensitive, gentle, lovable, had unraveled and revealed me to myself and proved the truth of the words that the way to find our true selves is sometimes through others unlike our true selves.

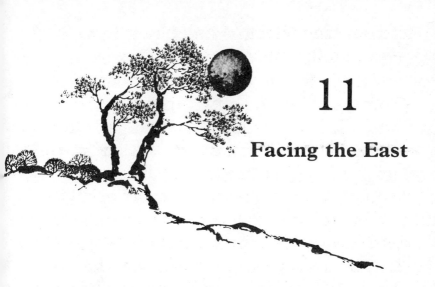

11

Facing the East

Deep peace of the running wave to you
Deep peace of the flowing air to you
Deep peace of the quiet earth to you
Deep peace of the shining stars to you
Deep peace of the Son of Peace to you
Celtic Blessing

JACK'S death was the celebration of a great mystery but it was also the celebration of his life, the life of a good man, reaching its peak in the moment of victory you have so intimately shared. I have forced myself to relive events in these pages and through this painful sharing something deep and wonderful has happened in me. The person who began the exercise and the person who finished it are altogether different. *Journey* best describes this process of being mysteriously made over, like the sunbeam that refracts through the various densities it encounters. Bending ever more toward the perpendicular my life will go on and on till I and It are one.

Perhaps it was my resolution to spend time in daily prayer ... I don't know. But with prayer for my only refuge I have been more fortunate than I could ever realize or be sufficiently grateful for. The past is too precious to write off and forget. By returning to it with fortitude and gratitude one can distill the last drop of purified wisdom and see things fall into place detail by detail without any waste.

I am finally through with running away from the pain and with intellectualizing my running away. Now, four years later, I have acknowledged and come to terms with my feelings. If I were to write a long letter to Jack's family in Holland again, as I did three years ago, I would not talk about the course I was giving and the other activities I was involved in, which meant nothing to them. I would let the pain come through.

Jack and I did not pretend, either to ourselves or to each other, about the gravity of his condition, but I have often asked myself whether things might have gone better for him if we had. It is a loaded question, the case for truth as opposed to benevolent deception, but our knowledge of the truth never prevented our maintaining hope—hope of remission, hope of partial recovery, hope of an outright cure or miracle.

Sooner or later however no one can escape the fact that for you or him now life might be coming to an end. Then there is need for a far greater and more important hope. The hope of dying in peace with all the burdens gone, all the hurts forgiven, all the damaged relationships put right as far as is humanly possible. The hope of happiness in the new dimension, and of love and welcome. Divine Hope.

After all, how long can you go on pretending death is not approaching even if you do pretend? But while we did not pretend, I deceived myself we were facing it together. The truth is that while Jack knew he was dying I was fussing like a toy, determined to make him better and so widening the isolating gulf between life and death, between him and me. It was only two days before his death that I really accepted there would be no miracle of the kind I had been praying for and we were on the same wavelength, but by then there was no need for words. We both knew. And time had run out.

Acceptance is a word much misunderstood. There is nothing passive about it and to do it one has to actively surrender and continually surrender. I think Jack knew from the beginning that he wouldn't make it and every few weeks when he had to go to his doctor to have his sickness-benefit form filled in he would say time was running out. He knew he wasn't fit to go back to work and he was so anxious about how he would have to go and look for a contract when the two weeks or a month were up. I have even tortured myself with the thought that possibly I further broke his spirit by suggesting he give up painting as being too risky for his lungs—at that time we knew nothing of the tumor.

I understood the psychology of keeping the sickness benefit short-term from the point of view of keeping up his morale and giving him the incentive to go back to work, but I found it very hard to forgive it once he was dead because he was too sick to have to carry the burden of such a worry. The tumor in his brain was secretly growing—and he was wondering how he would get a job.

After Jack was gone I followed up my emotional rejection of the house by overreacting against smoking and removing every single ashtray, and for a whole year nobody who visited me dared to smoke in my presence. If even a stranger lit up anywhere near me I would say that it made me cringe because my husband had died of lung cancer. I also got hold of and had mounted a Van Gogh print, *Skull with a Burning Cigarette*, put out by the National Heart Foundation of New Zealand. But what was the use? If the whole world stopped smoking it still wouldn't bring him back.

Why did this happen to me? I was saying in effect. But life is not long enough to answer the question *why*? One needs new eyes and a new heart to grasp the entirety of the plan.

One day when we have reorganized our lives to have more meaning we might then say, Blessed be the upheaval that set me free ... free from my rut ... free from looking upon my rut as the ultimate heaven and so perpetuating me in the possession of my petty hell ... free from my clutter, from my hangups, from myself.

To those who see the gift of life through the wonder of a child's eyes, life is exciting and joyful even in the midst of suffering. Children can hoot with amusement on a garbage heap as if they were in Disneyland, unaware that their insides teem with five kinds of worms, unconcerned that their mother has to scavenge to feed them.

Life must be lived because it is worth living. When it has been shattered it must somehow be *rebuilt*—or is a human life to be accorded less value in reconstruction than a mere work of art that has been vandalized, even if considered priceless?

———————————

Two paintings very special and dear to me and that have great significance for me are somehow bound up with this theme of change, of old to new, of death to life. One was done by Gay, the other by Jack.

Gay's painting was presented to me the Christmas before Jack's death and one month before we discovered he had cancer. We had it hanging in the passageway just outside our bedroom (until I later took it down at her request)—vivid, stunning, completely arresting, a little masterpiece. A strange creation in blues, whites, emeralds, purples and blacks about the mutations that could result from humanity's mistreatment of planet earth, though she was thinking more of pollution than of nuclear war, and she painted it for me because I fancied the theme and a smaller version of it she had done for a local art exhibition. This painting is prophetic—it depicts what could happen if this mindless abuse of Nature continues, Gay wrote in her description of it.

And prophetic indeed it was. It's all there, the disembodied eyes shedding helpless tears, the skeletal and visceral forms, the blue asphyxiated lungs, the skull, and above all, the Brain. Two skeleton hands offer a weeping eye. . . .

Now this painting was a work of love and so there was nothing in it that could have harmed or distressed me. Yet as I look at it I know he isn't "dead"—this isn't Jack. It isn't even the dying agonies of a wounded earth, its beauty ravaged beyond recognition and destroyed beyond hope of repair. A whole new dimension is missing from this painting, horrifyingly beautiful though it is, something to lift it out of its symbols of death into the rarefied stratosphere of the coming of Light . . . a healing of the wounds of earth and of the wounds of life.

God works this miracle all the time, the recovery he brings about far more incredible than the propensity for decay inherent in our selfishness. Anyone who doubts this should read the Book of Jonah. Only two pages long but *what pages*!

Whatever the controversiality of the details, the message scintillates like crystal, making it, to me, a most heart-warming example of God's tenderness and humor. There are limits to the way he puts up with our adolescent cheek but he does go to great lengths on a one-to-one basis to help us to understand the why and the wherefore. God wasn't only converting Nineveh and the Hebrews, he was converting Jonah!

The other painting, Jack's, was also prophetic. I spread the old shower curtain on the carpet in the rumpus room so the mess wouldn't be too bad and Jack donned his overalls, set up his easel and lit his pipe. He had only recently taken to a pipe and I was always scolding him about the ash he dropped around and, horrors, the holes he had burnt in his shirt! (If only I had mountains of ash round me now it would be the most heavenly sight in the world because he would be here for me to scold again.)

With a look of great importance Jack

started working and I watched the painting take shape. The thought in his mind was so big. He tried to put it into words for me but stupidly I didn't write them down. He looked so contented, puffing away at his pipe. We fooled ourselves we had stolen a march on destiny by substituting the pipe for cigarettes. Didn't the thick dark smear sticking to his ashtray prove the pipe trapped tar?

As Jack worked, delicately, almost hesitantly, a large cross emerged on a background impearled with squares of the gentlest grays, creamiest whites and palest golds. Within it, interlocking shapes in shades of brown, sepia, amber, yellow, coral, ochre, formed a jeweled jigsaw—people, Jack told me, people, finding their place in the scheme of things, no two alike, either in what they had been given or in what they had given back, yet somehow all united in this cosmic pageant of iridescent and living wonders because they are all inside the cross.

Jack didn't know it, but, without knowing any scripture or theology, the symbolical composition he dreamed up shows the New Testament teaching on reconciliation between God and man through the Son (Colossians 1:20) which he had never read.

———————————

As we are born whether we like it or not, so we die whether we like it or not, though in between we have a lot of say about the all-important choice *for* or *against* love, despite choice-limiting factors such as conditioning, temperament, life-situation and so on. That little bit of freedom is what ensures we are not stereotyped. I want to die as I was born: without the psychological fear of the unknown, or protest against the experience. With full confidence that I will not be alone. The tiny ant larva has thousands of nurses milling around to help it hatch from the cocoon, so why not I, who claim the whole family of the blessed as my own?

When crisis is present, so is immediate grace. The fetus who refused to be born out of fear of the unknown would never know its mother's kiss, its father's arms, the splash of rain, a bird riding the wind;

colors, music, love, humanness. And if dying, soon over like birth, is the only way to become a totally BE-ing person, who would not welcome it when the time came? I would. I would again, even though life in my body-state is precious and meaningful and I experience the paradox of relinquishment: to want and not want (death) at the same time.

The more I identify myself with Goodness by choice, consciously rejecting horror, for example, as being interesting or entertaining, the more I am aware of the fearful coexistence of Evil. Heaven and hell walk the same earth, breathe the same air, inhabit the same body. But in our present dimension of dulled perception we can have no true understanding of what they mean. Speaking for myself, I had to *realize* my own need of inner redemption before I even began to understand....

The various reported psychic experiences in states of consciousness where time-space laws no longer apply, especially concerning return from clinical death, confirm my belief that science itself will lead people back to faith in

God and survival beyond death—if they ever lost it. Wasn't it Pasteur who said that a shallow knowledge of science disposed a person to atheism but a deep wading in it disposed one to believe?

I think again of the Jonah story and of the Star of Bethlehem. God *loved* the world so much that he sent his only Son to live among us—loved not simply the god-fearing and decent but the *world*, just as it is reported by the news media in all its shattering starkness. Once more it is as if God is saying to all the Jonahs of this world and the pessimists and prophets of doom and end-of-the-world mongers:

> And am I not to feel sorry for Nineveh, the great city, in which there are more than a hundred and twenty thousand people who cannot tell their right hand from their left, to say nothing of all the animals? (Jonah 4:11).

To me Jack's painting also illustrates the *many mansions* of John (14:2), meaning rooms or dwelling places "waiting in heaven for others besides myself."[1] Not mutually exclusive compartments based on holiness, discrimination according to spiritual class in a stratified heaven, but room enough for everybody. Jesus is saying goodbye to his friends the night before his death and promising they will see him again because his Father's house is large enough for others besides himself and he is not going to live in it alone. He wants his loved ones round him. Heaven is, above all, home. And in a home there are no "places." All are equal and happy and beloved.

We all know what it is to carry the person loved in our hearts as part of us; "mutual indwelling" it has called, going right back to Aristotle's profound treatise *On Friendship*. Jesus speaks of the vine and the branches and of abiding in his love. The abiding place is the heart. There love is at rest. Its place is secure.

Heaven for me would be to meet God in *his* heart at last after a lifetime of only meeting him in mine. I am not rehearsing any speech to make because I do not know the prayer of ecstasy. That prayer will be a new one. Wordless. Timeless.

With it the tears inside my soul will be forever dried.

As far as I am concerned I have never doubted that Jack and I will meet again and that he sees me even now in some mysterious way and knows I am writing this book because of him. Wherever his place and my place will be, I know it will be *our place*.

We who by holy marriage became one body for the time of our mortal lives, and whose faith was tested and proved like gold by fire so that it may endure, are now through our shared experience fused into one heart and soul. Our true friendship has just begun.

NOTES

1   This is from the Knox translation. Throughout this book I have tended to quote scripture from memory or to paraphrase various editions available to me: *The Jerusalem Bible*, the *Good News Bible*, the *Revised Standard Version* and *The Way—The Living Bible*.

12

"And They Showed Me the Greatest Honor"

You will forget your sufferings, remember them as waters that have passed away. Your life, more radiant than the noonday, will make a dawn of darkness.

Job 11:16–17

WHAT more can I say about Jack that can't be inferred from reading between the lines? What can any woman say about the man she loves? When you love someone you can go on talking about that person—Saint John had that feeling when he ended his gospel: The world itself would not be able to contain all the books that would have to be written about what Jesus said and did.

A few days before he died Jack said if he lived he would serve the church, and by this I think he meant he would donate his time. But he does live. And he has more than time. He has eternity.

About three months after his death I received a special grace and I am sure he had something to do with it. For 13 years or so I had neglected our Blessed Mother Mary and discarded the discipline of saying the daily Rosary because I wanted to break free from what I thought had become dead habit. Only when those years had passed could I look back and see that they were the most barren of my life.

I tried to begin again on a regular basis and couldn't. Something had gone that I couldn't put back and I was very unhappy about it. Then that particular day a woman was sharing with me. She had been through great spiritual difficulty but had "stuck to the Rosary." Those words suddenly bounced back at me and I straightaway knew not a single day would ever pass again without my praying it, however imperfectly.

Yesterday I was asked whether I would ever consider marrying again, and I can only answer enigmatically that I do and I don't, each for very good reasons. The state of marriage is a "community of love" and I wonder why I allow myself to remain single for another day. I would be wanted and needed again, and God knows I have great need of such comforting. On the other hand, I would not come to it alone. With me would be everything that is a part of me, and the man who would become my husband and lover must first of all be my friend, someone whose arm would be around me for my sake as much as for his.

I know, of course, that Jack has no need of anything anymore and, as with the garden and everything else where I was reluctant to make alterations I knew he wouldn't have liked, I now have to decide with common sense according to *my* need or greater good. Those first years it was as if I was physically in the grave too, as if I didn't have a body at all. Now I am happy to feel once again and to know that I can still love. All the same, I keep the romantic shutter very firmly down in my mind because I don't want a phantom lover. I live with the cold fact that I have no one to love and no one loves me—yes, there is universal love and brotherly love, platonic love and divine love. But no human love.

In the field of human relationships it is often the ambiguous ones that play the most deepening part in shaping our self-hood, and I have found this to be true of God. For God resides in ambiguity.

Take every case of doubt multiplied by proliferating human error, and you have *nothing* to compare with the ambiguity surrounding God! To his critics this is unreconcilable with divinity; to his friends it is an aspect of the mystery of faith. I personally think God hides because he is a lover. Lovers enjoy throwing out hints, playing games with each other, putting on disguises and being coy. Ambiguity is one of the most exciting things about falling in love. You know, yet you don't know.

But in silence and darkness his Spirit still passes over the void—our world-crowded mess and unending chaos. And he still brings all things out of nothing—heartwarming wonders from the dregs of human experience. It would be so easy for him to chip in and do everything for us since he is all-powerful, but for that very reason he holds back to allow us scope for the common sense and good will he himself has given us, knowing that our stressful labor is bearing hidden fruit and one day we will be proud to hear him say: Well done.

I don't know how you feel about unexplained phenomena like luck, chance, and meaningful coincidence, but I have come to regard them as the spouting out in all directions of a very personal love; little fun-loving, perfectly timed treasure-hunt notes strewn hither and yon letting us know there's something there.

Something, Someone, is there *for me*, so whether I marry again or don't is not really what matters. What matters is to fulfil Jack's dying bargaining by the deeper commitment of my own life. The prayer I prayed aloud at his funeral, to know my life's work and to do it, also implies learning to become the kind of person God wants me to be in the years ahead—if years they are to be.

I know till this book is completed there cannot be another step. I also know its destiny is beyond my control. Nothing can take away from me the conviction that something is meant to come of all this, else why has it all happened and why have I been given the driving desire to write as well as the opportunity? I cannot believe God is making a mock of me. I know if I don't use the gift I will lose it.

Over the past few years there have been unmistakable nudges from the powers that be, some of them quite dramatic, which kept me going in spite of weariness and semidiscouragement when it seemed I was getting nowhere.

But of all the guidance I received the most incredible happened just as I was about to begin polishing my work. I awoke that morning with excruciating backache—I, who didn't know the meaning of the word! Then, the treatment I dreaded: repeated trips to the hospital for physiotherapy. I was somewhat bored foraging in a carton of donated magazines with nothing more startling than old digests and women's weeklies. But on the fifth day of my treatment I really took notice. Sitting right on top of the pile so that I couldn't *not* see it, in all its hardcover glory and virtually brand new, was *The Australian and New Zealand Writers Handbook* containing everything I needed to know but hadn't thought to research! I offered them two of my paperbacks in exchange and they graciously accepted the barter. Glory be. The assault on my back was fully worth the gain.

To feel something or experience something and then try to put it into words on the scale of a book are two different things, as anyone who has tried this disciplining and draining foolhardiness knows. Worse than the interrupted sleep and the cold arm is the ever-present fear of using other people's words or ideas that may have seeped into your subconscious through overexposure to the media. Time and again I discarded what I wrote because when I read it over a number of times it began to sound as if I had heard it somewhere and the words by then were sickeningly familiar. Time and again I became confused and lost confidence.

Now I see how fortunate it was I so often felt like Peter on the water . . . as if I were sinking . . . and that I was made so painfully aware that I haven't any of the cleverness associated with writing. It gives me the right degree of detachment and it makes this little book solely a work of love as there is no intrinsic worth to dull its meaning. To experience the fullness of the miracle and *walk* on a shipwrecking sea is far more terrifying than to know how lost and helpless one is. I, for one, am much more comfortable not to know what has been done and is being done for me and through me.

One day I had positive proof (if such a scientific term can be used of a faith experience) that God himself was at the bottom of all that was happening to me. There was an afternoon film on television I particularly wanted to put my feet up and watch. In former days I would have done just that, but this time I decided to sound God's feelings on the matter.

And what would *you* like, Lord? All right ... if you *are* listening, and you *don't* want me to watch it, let the telephone ring *the moment* the program comes on. I switched on the set, and as the program came on the telephone rang. I ran to answer it with goose bumps and so out of breath that the caller wondered what had happened.

How could I have said, God has just spoken to me? But it was exactly as if Jesus was saying: Leave the dead to bury their dead. Just get on with the job, Shirley.

For all the wonderfulness of a thing like this, God does not always answer so promptly and clearly. His usual way is to let us exercise common sense, initiative and decision, for there is always the possibility of deception and misguidance if we are lacking in discernment. But once in a while there is a mysterious urge within us to act in a certain way or to make a specific prayer because at that moment God intends to surprise us with a little wonder for our reassurance and encouragement. I experienced this a number of times in regard to my beloved dead—they are closer than we could ever realize.

One morning there was a preciously uplifting encounter with Jack. I woke wanting *to hear* the words "I love you" and I told him so. But the radio, dialed from end to end, gave me nothing, not even a third-rate love song. Then, for no apparent reason, I was making a sudden, desperate effort to get to the 9 a.m. Mass (I usually walk down to the evening one). Within 20 minutes I was showered, dressed, away on my bicycle. I arrived just as the dear old priest was delivering the homily pinpointing the words I was meant to hear as he quoted a poem where "I love you—I love you—I love you" occurred at least half a dozen times!

Then there was the little exchange with my dear Jesuit spiritual father who had given me a copy of his translation into English of a great Sanskrit epic, no small achievement for a European. But I had not read it to date. One day when I was touchingly reproaching him for having died before I could share this book of mine with him, I ventured to say: If you can see it now, I want to know. Instantly there were words in my consciousness which I could not have put there: You will find the answer on page 26 of *my* book. I rushed to the bookshelf and believe it or not, *there was no page 26*! It was the only page without a number and it had been bound in upside down! He was laughing at me! Telling me off for not having read it!

And so our hearts remain in wonder at the daily miracles of our lives. Daily miracles no longer surprise me. And once we have had an insight into the paradox of God's amazing grace, there is only one response worthy of the gift: we must share it, share it, share it.

So many memories of Jack come flooding in that I want to record but for the sake of brevity must treat selectively:

Jack—sitting at our little Hammond organ playing *Blowing in the Wind* (his first and only piece, his theme tune and a triumph for him) with *all* of his fingers, the two little ones fanned out, his mouth open and the most puckered concentration on his face, but he is really making melody. If I tell them, darling, about the week I spent teaching you, you will fabricate the biggest fib of your life— She rapped me over the knuckles! But I persevered. For a whole week he didn't know what I was talking about, then suddenly it registered. He had found the missing link between the keyboard and the score!

Jack—all donned up in his overalls painting the sun porch at the back of the house and kissing me in the middle of it, and our little joke about the neighbors wondering *What's going on there?*

Jack—telling me during our friendship days that I was such a challenge to him because I was so unpredictable (when I was trumping up some excuse to get ride of him) and also saying very assertively once we were married: We're not going! That's all there is to it! but clearly aching to be persuaded.

Jack—supporting children for World Vision (the correspondence done by me, who else—my tears splashing down all over the Bengali script when little Bawilian's letter came from Bangladesh).

Jack—receiving my first wedding anniversary present, a light-weight dressing gown with matching briefs in his favorite colors laboriously made for him amid great secrecy and stealth to take on our overseas trip. He brushed it aside and I was almost hurt—and then I understood. These little acts of love were too much for him. They had to become a comfortable part of his environment before he could take notice of them.

Jack—"helping" me to change the sheets on our double bed and invariably provoking my ire by tugging them the wrong way!

Jack—surrounded by family in Holland and the two of us making plans about having them here for holidays in turn. I bought recipe books galore—I'll become a super chef. Darling, the guest room is lying empty, do you know?

Jack—having his first taste of Asia and learning a healthy respect for it from a rather nasty experience. The sun was boring into our pores and in his innocence and ignorance he took refuge under a tree. It was only the casual glance I tossed him that saved him. Within minutes he had begun to crawl with large red ants. In my panic I began to scold him as I dragged him away from under the tree shouting, *Look at the ants*! He panicked too and started stamping around. I could see by his face he didn't think much of Singapore! By then he had had enough both of the ants and of me.

Also in Singapore at the Instant Asia Cultural Show (opposite the Tiger Balm Garden) he refused to be cooperative and have a photo taken with a cobra round his neck in the snake charmer's booth. *You* have a go, he said rather testily, and I must admit I wasn't very cooperative either!

His lung was already the unhappy cradle of an infant of prey and doom, and neither of us knew it. No hint of anything amiss except our general travel weariness. Once home I set to work industriously making all the albums of all our memories....

How we were looking forward to our future home after the sale of our properties. How I would enjoy keeping house for him. But there would be another move involving only him. There was a plot of earth marked out for him and he was on his way to another home.

Jack—in his blotched overalls, more grey than white from all the jobs well done, high on a roof humming the familiar tuneless, toneless, wordless song he always sang when satisfied with life. What is it, darling? he greeted me at the work site. Big smile. (Oh, thank heaven for my dark glasses hiding my swollen eyes.) Come down first and I'll tell you. It's the doctor. He wants to see us both—together.

Jack—in the hospital, first Napier, then Wellington, and how he broke down and wept like a child before his admission because he realized he was really on his own from then on. Five weeks after surgery with me by his side, thinking of earthquakes and of him with those wires and tubes....

Then our priest's visit when business took him to the capital and how Jack broke down at its unexpectedness. The same when Paul and Ali altered their holiday route and came. Weekend visits too from Raewyn and her husband motoring all the way from Napier. Then our final hopeless trip to Palmerston North Hospital for further cobalt perhaps . . . for a little extra time perhaps . . . knowing all the while this was really the end.

You have left me so *rich*. You have given me the moon by night and the sun by day. You have dressed me in all the colors of the rainbow, filled my arms with an ever-glowing bouquet of fragrances. You have taken me apart and put me together again and *I* am your work of art.

You endowed me with undreamt-of possessions when you publicly declared:

I, Jacobus, take you, Shirley. . . .

One day I will open the plastic bag that has your letters. That first one that did the grand mile from Taradale to Greenmeadows and told me shyly: I don't think, but I know I love you, Shirley. And the others from the hospital on top of the daily telephone calls that said how much you missed me. And the last.

Such a wonderful thing happened one day at the cemetery, not long after Jack's death. A couple stood beside a new grave close by and she was crying. We got talking and then we said a little prayer together after which we embraced.

Presently I looked back at Jack's plaque and what did I see? I could hardly believe my eyes. At the very moment I turned to look I saw a little yellow-hammer fly down like an alighting butterfly to the center of the space on the plaque reserved for my particulars when I die, as the grave is meant for two. At the top of the headstone, which is lying flat down, it tells about Jack; at the bottom are the words: HAPPY ARE THEY WHO ARE CALLED TO THE LORD'S SUPPER. And in the empty space between sits this tiny glorious creature lighting up the dark gray slab like a little love song.

I couldn't take my eyes off it. It preened its feathers . . . wings . . . breast . . . then it tucked its head under its wing and went to sleep. It stayed 15 minutes and only flew away when I made a move to go. There were *four* people standing only a few yards away and the late morning was drenched in sunshine, yet it *went to sleep* without any fear, and, with the whole cemetery to choose from, it was on *Jack's* plaque in *my* space.

I had to turn away. The image was too moving to receive except only the little I could bear. Just a few days earlier at the sacrament of reconciliation our priest told me the image he kept getting was that of a helpless little bird and a strong, loving, protective God. And he prayed I might have hope. Now, blinded by tears, not for Jack's mortal remains lying in the earth at my feet, but for the tenderness enfolding me, I had to move quickly away.

Thy kingdom come, thy will be done. In my heart. In the world. How can I not trust when the Lord is speaking to me everywhere I turn? Slowly I must let go of everything that isn't his perfect love. From now on I must be accountable only to the Truth within me.

———————

Today the grief came up again in a wave—nothing new, just the unbearable memory of the "I hate you" I had shouted out in anger—and I turned to Jack's picture and prayed: Comfort me. Comfort me. Dürer's *Sketchbook* came into my mind. I opened it and this line caught my eye: "A really splendid meal was prepared and they showed me the greatest honor."

As I stared at it the drab print took on the glory of illuminated manuscript and in its light I saw the full rotation.... Day had to become night before it could be day again. I knew then that the fellowship service I had arranged in which Jack had shared fully at the communion table for the first time, and in the presence of so many friends, had been my greatest act of love for him, greater even than the writing of this book. In fact it is the foundation on which this book was written.

He is a cherished guest at a banquet, young and healthy like a boy again, rejoicing with unutterable and exalted joy, a joy so glorious that it cannot be described. He departed this life reflecting God's life and love. The "new" life. No one could ask more. Sadness and death are taken away and they will never come back because the world of the past has gone.

No, we are never left uncomforted. Once we have grieved fully we are helped to put grief aside as no longer serving any purpose because its bitterness has given way to triumph and enlightenment. Now it is up to us to radiate the newborn joy and to pass on the comfort we received from prayer, from books, from the kindness of others, and from our own resolution to live fully once more.

God is already wiping away the tears from the eyes of all people of good will as he raises to himself everywhere a new humanity determined to counter hate with love. So many wonderful things are happening that sometimes I feel earth and its sufferings are like snowflakes dissolving into a dazzling Sun.

Despite the ever-present growing evil, the sparkles from this radiance are everywhere and I thank God I am part of it. Just as a little bird who has found a song pours it out while unaware that you are listening, so someone is listening to your life's music too. But you sing sweeter if you know, and you sing for him. Blessed little moments ... putting touches of ecstasy into everyday life. Delight in a pretty dress, or in hair that is what it was meant to be, a woman's glory. Thankfulness too big for human language. Openness to laughter as well as to tears. And the strange and bewildering moment when you know you can fall in love again. As one moment rises to the next and the next, there will suddenly be a moment which is a moment no longer but the beautiful glow of the ever-breaking Dawn of the utmost eternities.

How much I needed the strengthening, the uplifting, this comfort to anoint me, because now there is only the silence.

SILENCE....

Everywhere I turn—Jack's silence and mine, sometimes even God's. I learn now to unsay words—the silence does not need them. But the tears I weep I know will be wiped away.

May he keep you facing the East, knowing the dawn will come.

It seems so long since dear Jack left us. I prayed for you both, but more for you since he is fully Alive, while you are still growing in the Mystery.

Our priest's words, years old in time, are beyond time in my memory. May he keep you likewise. And thank you.

No need for you now to hurt when you read this and be angry again with the God of everything because of the pain of love. If peace is the beginning of dawn, then the dawn *has come*.

I have shared with gratitude and humility the miracle that we received. For each one of us is a miracle. And each one has a miracle to share.

Epilogue

DARLING, *I have written it.*

And as I prepare to clear the mess off my mistreated dining table and put away my typewriter, I make a little prayer, I offer this work to the Lord, not for any intrinsic worth as being the most important of my life, but as being the most loving. With humility I ask a blessing on it. I hope it will speak to the heart of each one who reads it, for it was written from the heart.

I have written it for those who suffer. May they be taught by their suffering and may their tears of love overflow in gratitude and break into mother-of-pearl.

I have written it for those who cannot suffer, because they will not let themselves. May they meet someone who will gently show them how. We are made for happiness and we need to be happy, but our happiness on this earth is bound up with others and in that lies the essence of

our suffering and the source of our purification. Eventually it will be bound up
with happiness itself, and then we will be
beyond all need and all desire.

I have written it for myself, in the
hope it may put back into our world
some of the love I have received. The
wind of the Spirit can illumine and
multiply all these world-wide sparks
till they are stars ... STARS ...
STARS....

But most of all I have written it for
you, and there is no need to tell you why.
Remember how I used to make up little
verses for your birthday?

Here is the last of them, from me, your
Shirley.

This little book of no consequence
Comes with silent offering
Like ancient gold, myrrh,
 frankincense
That once were offering for a King.
Praised be my Lord God with all his
creatures; and especially our brother
the sun who brings us the day....
Saint Francis of Assisi—
the rapturous Hymn to Creation